# The
# BOTTOMLINE

# on ROI

*Basics, Benefits, & Barriers to Measuring*
*Training & Performance Improvement*

# The
# BOTTOMLINE

# on ROI

*Basics, Benefits, & Barriers to Measuring
Training & Performance Improvement*

Patricia Pulliam Phillips

**CEP Press**
A wholly owned subsidiary of
The Center for Effective Performance, Inc.
*Atlanta, Georgia*

International Society for
Performance Improvement
*Silver Spring, Maryland*

**OTHER BOOKS PUBLISHED BY CEP PRESS**

*How to Make Smart Decisions About Training,*
  *by Paul G. Whitmore, Ph.D.*

*Analyzing Performance Problems, Third Edition,*
  *by Robert F. Mager & Peter Pipe*

*Making an Impact, by Timm J. Esque*

*Conquering Organizational Change: How to Succeed Where Most*
  *Companies Fail, by Pierre Mourier & Martin Smith, Ph.D.*

For more information, contact:
CEP Press
2300 Peachford Rd.
Suite 2000
Atlanta, GA 30338
www.ceppress.com
(770) 458-4080 or (800) 558-4CEP

Library of Congress Cataloging-in-Publication Data
Phillips, Patricia Pulliam.
    The bottom line on ROI : basics, benefits, & barriers to measuring /
Patricia Pulliam Phillips ; editor, Jack Phillips.
        p. cm.
Includes bibliographical references and index.
    ISBN 1-879618-25-7 (alk. paper)
    1. Employees—Training of—Cost effectiveness. 2. Rate of return. I.
Phillips, Jack J., 1945- II. Title.
    HF5549.5.T7 P436 2002
    658.3'12404—dc21
                                        2001008601

Printed in the United States of America

09 08 07 06 05 04 03 02 10 9 8 7 6 5 4 3 2 1

# Contents

Foreword                                                                 7

Acknowledgments                                                         15

Chapter 1: **The Need for ROI**                                         17

Chapter 2: **Who Should Use ROI**                                       35

Chapter 3: **Building a Credible Process:
    The Evaluation Puzzle**                                             43

Chapter 4: **The ROI Methodology**                                      59

Chapter 5: **Stage 4: The Communication Process Model**                 81

Chapter 6: **Overcoming Barriers and the Next Steps**                   95

Appendix                                                               101

References                                                             107

Index                                                                  111

ROI Methodology Model Insert                                  Back of Book

# Foreword

## THE REALITIES OF ROI

It is my pleasure to introduce this first book in the new Measurement in Action Series, *The Bottomline on ROI*. The Measurement in Action Series aims to provide the latest tools, practical research, and 'how to' advice on measuring and evaluating a wide variety of programs—from e-learning to corporate universities. This book takes the first steps toward that goal by offering a look at the true *bottomline* on return on investment, or ROI.

The term ROI often inspires a variety of images, ideas, and concerns. Some professionals are frightened by the notion of evaluating ROI for training and development, performance improvement, or human resources. They have anxiety about how the ROI may be interpreted and used. For those professionals, however, who are open to learning about the ROI methodology and its benefits, ROI can be an opportunity, a challenge, and a tool to improve programs and solutions. While some debate its appropriateness, others are quietly and deliberately pursuing ROI in a variety of settings—and they are achieving impressive results.

ROI is not for everyone or every organization. Some organizations lack the trust and supportive climate that ROI requires. The successful champion of ROI must be willing to learn, change, and try new things—using ROI as a process improvement tool. Without this attitude and approach, it may be best not to try.

*The Bottomline on ROI* gives you the information you need to use

ROI to your advantage and become that advocate.

ROI is growing in prominence and popularity, and people are asking questions to decide if it is right for their organizations. There is a need for information. Barriers to the implementation of ROI do exist. But there are ways to address and eliminate these barriers and achieve success with ROI. In my experience, I've observed some realities about ROI that I'd like to share with you. These realities reflect the drivers behind this book, and illustrate some of the challenges that an advocate will face. The stage is set for training and performance improvement executives who can accept the realities and challenges of ROI and use it to reach their goals.

## ROI REALITY #1

While there are many applications and implementations, several issues are inhibiting the widespread use of the ROI methodology. Although there are some realistic barriers, most of these inhibitors are myths, based on misunderstandings of the process and what it can achieve.

As a tool, ROI does not currently enjoy widespread dominate application. This is discouraging given the value of the process. Most individuals involved in ROI implementation attend ROI certification workshops with a great deal of built-in resistance. They're driven by their senior team or by ultimatums from the top executive group. They resist all the way. This is due, in part, to fear of the unknown and fear of what ROI will do, particularly if it is negative. There is concern that a negative ROI might bring an end to their programs or their jobs. This concern is often based on misunderstanding and lack of knowledge. A comment from the audience at a keynote presentation at the International Conference of the American Society for Training and Development underscores this concern: "I transferred to the training and development function to escape numbers and, ultimately, the accountability that goes along with them. Now it looks like we have to face the same type of numbers here." That comment drew a round of applause. This comment illustrates the common fear of anything number-based.

*The Bottomline on ROI* explores and dispels the myths about ROI that challenge its use. These fears and misconceptions may often act as barriers, but they don't have to inhibit ROI application and implementation. Some very real barriers do exist. The ROI methodology will require additional time, costs, and new skills to bring change to the design, development, and implementation of solutions. But when the payoff of ROI is considered, the benefits exceed the investment, usually by large amounts.

## ROI REALITY #2

*The Bottomline on ROI* is client-driven, based on a quest to understand more about the ROI methodology and its potential payoff. Prospective clients need more information on the benefits of implementing ROI.

*The Bottomline on ROI* was developed in response to the needs of clients. Organizations pursuing ROI have asked for more detail on the business realities of ROI. They want to know the actual monetary value of the ROI methodology so they can know, up front, what to expect in terms of payoff.

Potential clients have always addressed this issue during initial inquiries. "What's the bottom line?" they would say. "Show me why we should pursue this. Show me some of the key concerns and issues so that we can make a decision." To understand what the ROI methodology can achieve, potential clients need to clarify issues, terms, and concepts that are very basic to understanding the process. This book accomplishes that.

## ROI REALITY #3

This unique book is an indispensable guide for exploring ROI with the ultimate goal of deciding if it is right for the organization. It is a 'must read' for anyone interested in ROI.

This book accomplishes several important objectives:

1. Increase understanding of the ROI concept, assumptions, and methodology. It is a quick reference for the ROI methodology.

2. Identify who's using the ROI methodology and why, and in what type of applications. It is important to see who is—and is not—embracing this process improvement tool.

3. Provide the information necessary to make a decision about ROI. This is a very critical issue! Most people explore the ROI methodology with this question: "Is this right for us? Is this needed in our organization at this time?" This book provides the information needed to make this critical decision.

4. Increase reader understanding and appreciation of the ROI methodology, including the vast contributions it can make. It will also help them understand how the process has been utilized to add value in organizations and continues to add value.

5. Dispel the significant inhibiting ROI myths that get in the way of a successful application and implementation.

6. Help plot the next steps. If the decision is to move forward with the process, the obvious question is, "What's next?" This publication explores some of the next steps.

This book is not a detailed reference on the ROI methodology—others do a very good job of presenting the process. This book does not dwell on case studies—others are available for that purpose. This book is not about tools, templates, and techniques—others serve as a resource for application and implementation. Instead, it is a book about how to *understand and make sense of the ROI methodology from a business perspective.*

## ROI REALITY #4

The ROI methodology is being implemented globally in all types of organizations for all types of programs. Many training and development, organizational development, performance improvement, and human resource professionals are using the ROI methodology to radically change the way they design, develop, and deliver programs and solutions.

From almost any vantage point, applications of the ROI methodology have grown significantly in number. Hundreds of organizations in all types of settings all across the globe are now using the ROI methodology. It is proving to be a valuable performance improvement tool, and the converts are rapidly pouring in. After speaking at a recent conference, I overheard the training manager for a large manufacturing company make this statement: "We don't believe in ROI, and we have a policy stating we will not use the ROI methodology." Less than a year later, two individuals from the same organization attended one of our certification workshops. When I asked about their plans, they commented, "We've decided to implement the ROI methodology throughout our training and development organization. We have a goal to move quickly." It is not unusual to see this type of about-face. Unfortunately, too often the change is based on external pressures, creating an urgent situation.

Growth in the application of ROI has cut across all types of organizations and industries. When one major organization in an industry begins using it, others often become interested. For example, the three largest package delivery companies in the world have implemented this methodology, partly because their peers were using it. For the same reason, almost all major telecommunication companies in the US have implemented the methodology.

The ROI methodology has expanded globally and has been utilized in practically every country. My colleagues and I at the Jack Phillips Center for Research have been involved in its implementation in organizations in 35 countries.

The methodology has also moved into different sectors of

organizations. It began primarily in the manufacturing sector—the logical birthplace of any process improvement. It quickly moved to the service sector, then to non-profits and healthcare, and on to government organizations. We're now beginning to see applications in the educational sector, where schools and universities struggle to show the value of their programs.

Where initially the methodology was employed to show the impact of supervisor training, now it is used in all types of training programs, from highly technical programs to long-term executive development. Applications include coaching and management development programs, such as business coaching, mentoring, and career development. Human resources programs—such as orientation, compensation systems, recruiting strategies, employee relation initiatives, and retention solutions—have been evaluated successfully with the ROI methodology.

Finally, the number of individuals who have attended formal training in the methodology is staggering. Over 6,000 specialists and managers have attended almost 500 of our two-day workshops conducted in major cities throughout the world. A thousand individuals have been prepared to implement this internally through an ROI certification process. The numbers are continuing to grow rapidly.

## ROI REALITY #5

Sooner or later, every training and development, performance improvement, or human resource function will face increasing accountability and will have to address ROI. For some, the time is now. For others it may be long term, but it will eventually surface.

*The Bottomline on ROI* details many of the important influences responsible for the growth of ROI . Four significant ones are emphasized here:

➤ Globally, economic forces are making it necessary for all segments of an organization to show the payoff of all types of solutions and programs. Every function must make a contribution!

12

➤ The ROI is the ultimate level of evaluation, where the cost of the solution is compared to the monetary benefits of the solution. While other levels of evaluation are important, nothing tells the story quite like ROI, particularly for those sponsors and clients demanding a monetary payback.

➤ The ROI concept is familiar to most managers, particularly those with business school training. They see it as an important accountability tool. They've seen it applied in many other areas and welcome its use with training and development and other performance initiatives. They realize that it's not a fad—it is a proven technique that will be here for years to come.

➤ Top executives are requiring this type of measurement for new (and existing) programs. Previously, they hesitated to ask for ROI because they didn't realize it could be done. In some situations, they were told it's impossible to measure ROI for training, learning, human resources, and other 'soft issues.' Now, they're learning that it *can* be done, and they're requiring this level of evaluation.

## ROI REALITY #6

A new breed of performance improvement executive is achieving success with ROI. They are using the ROI methodology to show value as they operate with a business mindset. They are becoming business partners in the organization.

The good news: changes are being made and success is being achieved. A new breed of performance improvement executive is managing many training and development, performance improvement, and human resource functions. These new executives bring a business mindset to the table. They want to operate the function as an important business enterprise, as a major contributor, adding value to the business—using the ROI methodology to support that cause.

These new executives are choosing to be proactive instead of reactive when it comes to implementing the ROI methodology. They realize that they must take the lead and bring on change or it will not happen. ROI is being recognized as a necessary tool. In any functional part of a business, performance must be validated to be recognized as a contributor.

Finally, this new breed of performance improvement executive sees ROI as a challenge. It is not easy. It is difficult to apply this process to all of the different situations, scenarios, and environments where it must work to be a useful tool. They understand that it will take time to alter their practices and implement the methodology.

## Unique Perspective of the Author

Patti has utilized the training and development function throughout her career. As an operating executive, she was often reluctant to allow her employees to participate in training programs because she could see little value in them. When she first became aware of the ROI methodology, the overwhelming need for it was evident. She embraced the process and began marketing it to others. She quickly realized why others were interested and saw what they needed to help them move forward. She observed the payoff they got, sometimes helping them along the way.

Patti is an astute observer of the ROI methodology, having observed and learned from literally hundreds of presentations, consulting assignments, and engagements. In addition, she's an excellent researcher and student of the process—studying how it's developed and how it works. She's an excellent practitioner and an effective contributor to the ROI methodology through presentations, explanations, consulting, and advice. She's become an ROI expert in her own right. She brings this unique perspective—not as the individual who initially developed the process for applications in training and development, but as a person who has observed it, applied it successfully, and now lives with it in every way. I think you will enjoy this book. Let us know your reaction.

Jack J. Phillips
Author, *Return on Investment in Training and Performance Improvement Programs*

# Acknowledgments

No project, regardless of size and scope, is completed without the help and support of others. My sincere thanks go to all the people at CEP Press. They have been extremely supportive of this project, not only with this particular project, but with the launch of the Measurement in Action Series as well. Suzanne Bennett has been the greatest! She worked with me to ensure that we developed the first book of the new series in such a way that readers could get to the *bottomline*.

My thanks also go to my husband, Jack. Jack's unwavering support of my work is always evident. His idea for the Measurement in Action Series was to provide readers with a practical understanding of the various components of a comprehensive measurement and evaluation process. I hope this first book in the series sets the stage in the light he originally envisioned. *Thank you for being my biggest cheerleader!*

## CHAPTER 1

# The Need for ROI

Training and performance improvement *programs* typically represent from 1.3 percent to 13 percent of an organization's payroll (Galvin 2001). The total dollars budgeted represent an enormous investment in training. Approximately $57 billion was spent on training in the US in 2001, representing a 5 percent increase over 2000 (*Training* 2001). While an increase, it is not typical of industry patterns over the past several years. While some organizations are increasing training budgets, others are reducing budgets. These reductions have been due in part to training's inability to demonstrate value to the organization (Van Buren 2000).

The large expenditures and the need to show value are two of the primary drivers placing increased emphasis on the measurement and evaluation of training and performance improvement programs. Of the top five trends in the training and performance improvement field, increased emphasis on costs, implementation of comprehensive measurement and evaluation, and return on investment, or ROI, top the list (Phillips 1999; Willmore 2001).

The issue of ROI in training and performance improvement is rapidly growing in prominence. "ROI" appears in books, on conference agendas, and in training and performance improvement promotional and advertising materials. Rarely does a topic stir up emotions to the degree the ROI issue does. Some individuals characterize ROI as inappropriate for training and performance improvement; others passionately characterize ROI as the answer to their accountability concerns. The truth lies somewhere between these viewpoints. This book will help you determine how ROI can address accountability concerns in your organization.

## ROI: THE BASICS

The concept of ROI has been used for centuries (Sibbett 1997). The ROI calculation, earnings divided by investment, blends in one number all the major ingredients of profitability. The ROI statistic can be compared to other opportunities inside or outside the company, which makes it ideal for comparing training's impact on the organization to that of other investments. Practically, however, the ROI calculation alone is an imperfect measurement that must be used in conjunction with other performance measurements as part of a measurement and evaluation process (Hornegren 1982).

One of the earliest methods for evaluating training and performance improvement investments was the cost-benefit analysis process. The cost-benefit analysis compares the benefits of a program to its costs through a benefit-cost ratio (BCR) (Thompson 1980; Kearsley 1982; Nas 1996; Phillips 1997b). In formula form, the BCR calculation is:

$$BCR = \frac{\textbf{Program Benefits}}{\textbf{Program Costs}}$$

A benefit-cost ratio of one means that the benefits equal the costs. A benefit-cost ratio of two, written as 2:1, indicates that for each dollar spent on the program two dollars were returned as benefits.

ROI, on the other hand, compares the *net* program benefits and costs. The ratio is usually expressed as a percent by multiplying the fractional values by 100 (Phillips 1997a). The ROI formula is:

$$\text{ROI (\%)} = \frac{\text{Net Program Benefits}}{\text{Program Costs}} \times 100$$

Net benefits are program benefits minus program costs. The ROI value is related to the benefit-cost ratio by a factor of one—for example, a BCR of 2.45:1 is the same as an ROI value of 145 percent. This formula is essentially the same as ROI in other types of investments and is a term that's easily understood by executive management. The ROI calculation will be discussed later in more detail.

But as noted earlier, the ROI formula alone is insufficient. Other variables contribute to the ROI calculation and are important measures in reporting bottomline results. These variables include:

➤ Participant reaction and satisfaction with the program—not only the learning environment, but the level at which the environment, materials, and program facilitation contribute to the learning. Further, participant intent to use the learning, their perceived relevance of the programs, and the perceived value of the program can often provide predictive information regarding the learning and application of the skills (Alliger and Tannenbaum 1997; Warr, Allan, and Birdi 1999; APQC 2000);

➤ The degree of learning that takes place such that participants can apply the new skills/knowledge immediately following the program and so that the application of the new skills/knowledge becomes routine;

➤ The degree to which new skills and knowledge are applied on the job in order to influence business measures;

➤ The change in business measures as a result of the application of new skills and knowledge learned in the program.

Together these variables influence the ultimate monetary measure of program success, ROI.

Evaluation at this level of comprehensiveness, however, is more than just collecting and analyzing data. Comprehensive evaluation requires a means to ensure that results are credible and that the evaluation process can be replicated. The lack of credibility of results can quickly diminish any evidence of program impact. A variety of individuals should be able to use the same process to evaluate the same training program with similar results. Without this potential for replication, the evaluation process itself loses credibility. The entire measurement and evaluation process has to be assessed to ensure that it incorporates all of the key elements necessary to provide a credible process and credible results.

Prior to embarking on any level of evaluation, the training and performance improvement staff and management should ask themselves a simple question: "What is our intent in collecting these data?" Even if the only data collected are participant reaction, if there is no intent to analyze, communicate, and use the data collected, the entire effort is for naught. The organization will benefit more from conserving valuable resources than it will by using resources on data collection design and implementation and doing nothing with the data.

In recent years, ROI evaluation has been applied not only to training and performance improvements programs, but to human resources programs, change initiatives, and technologies (like e-learning and sales force automation) (Phillips and Phillips 2001). But selecting the appropriate program for this type of evaluation is critical. Not all programs are candidates for ROI. ROI evaluation can be an expensive and resource-consuming process, and careful planning is a necessity.

*The Bottomline on ROI* presents the rationale for developing and implementing a comprehensive measurement and evaluation process including ROI. The book presents and explores an evaluation process that is credible with key stakeholders. Implementing the ROI methodology generates a scorecard of balanced measures including participant reaction, satisfaction, and planned action, learning, application, impact, ROI, and intangible benefits. This scorecard provides a clear indication of the actual impact of training and performance improvement programs.

Whether seeking an initial understanding of ROI evaluation or looking for ways to generate support for ROI within an organization, this book provides readers a clear understanding of ROI and how it can be implemented. Included in this book are:

➤ Key issues driving the need to measure training and performance improvement programs;

➤ Benefits of developing ROI;

➤ Profile of organizations typically using ROI;

➤ Symptoms indicating an organization is ready for ROI;

➤ Pieces of the evaluation puzzle necessary to build a comprehensive measurement and evaluation system;

➤ Criteria for effective ROI implementation;

➤ The ROI methodology, a model that will produce a balanced set of measures;

➤ A communication process model for ensuring effective communication both during and after the process;

➤ Barriers to implementing the ROI methodology; and

➤ Steps to get started implementing the ROI methodology.

The book also includes checklists, tools, and templates along with a reference list to further enhance the reader's understanding and implementation of the ROI methodology.

## RATIONALE FOR IMPLEMENTING ROI

The rationale for focusing on ROI may be obvious, but it helps to further explore the various reasons why now is the time to pursue ROI. Training and performance improvement practices have existed for many years and are among the core activities of most medium-sized and large organizations. Traditionally training focused on technical skills. The predominant industry was manufacturing. Therefore, skills-based training was easily linked to productivity goals. Today, however, the service sector accounts for over 70 percent of total employment

(Malecki 1997). This shift from manufacturing to a service-intensive industry not only changed the product/service offerings, but brought on new issues including the management and development of organizations, teams, individuals, and information. These issues brought new challenges to the training arena. A much wider variety of training and performance improvement programs are offered now to address today's more complex issues. Training and performance improvement programs include technical skills training, management and leadership development, diversity awareness, and even wellness training. A new focus on issues such as customer satisfaction and job satisfaction has grown from the need to be competitive both for customers as well as employees.

Along with the change in training focus comes the issue of training delivery. Today the question is whether to use training facilitators or technology as a means to deliver training. Another question is whether to provide training within the organization or through an external training supplier. Of the $56.8 billion budgeted for training in 2001, $19.3 billion (34 percent) was designated for external training suppliers (*Training* 2001).

Along with these changes in training and performance improvement come changes in the way training is viewed by management. As previously mentioned, in the past production goals measured the success of training. Today, the "softer" issues can be more difficult to measure. For some time, there was an inherent belief that all training, including soft-skills training, was good for the organization. Today tangible evidence is required to show training's impact—even with the softest training programs. This tangible evidence comes through using a comprehensive measurement and evaluation process including ROI.

In addition to these trends, several specific issues are driving the current need to measure the results of training and performance improvement programs.

## Client Demands

Client demand is one of the most considerable influences in pursuing a comprehensive measurement and evaluation process including ROI. Clients—those funding the training and performance improvement programs—are requesting evaluation data, up to and including measuring the actual ROI (Gerson and McCleskey 1998). The two most commonly asked questions at the beginning of a program are: "How do I know if this program will pay off for us?" and "Will this represent an adequate return on my investment?" Although the accountability issue has always been present, it has never existed at today's heightened level. When the client demands results, the training and performance improvement function must explore and implement a process to provide those results. The process must be credible enough for the client to believe the results. Client questions and issues must be addressed in a simple, rational way. The client must be able to see the impact of the training program and be able to compare its impact with that of other processes and initiatives.

## Competition for Scarce Resources

Another critical reason to pursue an ROI methodology is to meet or beat the competition for scarce resources. Organizations have limited funding by which to operate. Given those limitations on funding, budget allocation can often become a competitive process. Various organization functions compete for resources in order to implement their specific programs, processes, and initiatives. If functions don't make efficient use of the resources they allocate, those resources will go elsewhere. Those functions showing the greatest evidence of impact on the organization often receive the largest amount of funding. This usually means an increase for one area at the expense of another. The resource allocation issue is a serious driver in providing ROI calculations of training and performance improvement programs.

## "At Risk" Funding

Some organizations put resources at risk by basing the allocation of resources on the actual monetary contribution of programs (Schmidt 1997). For example, annual budgets are placed at risk by basing them on a threshold ROI. If the minimum ROI is met for key training and performance improvement programs, the budget remains level. Exceeding the threshold results in increased budget; falling below the threshold causes a reduction of budget. This "pay for performance" process requires the use of an ROI methodology for training and performance improvement programs in order to secure increased resources.

## Consequences of Ineffective Programs

Ineffective programs bring additional scrutiny and skepticism onto the training and performance improvement function. Many training and performance improvement programs do not live up to their promises or expectations. They do not deliver the expected results—at least not in terms the client understands. When results are insufficient, concern often surrounds the credibility of the evaluation process, the program, and the overall function. As a result, greater restraints and demands are placed on the function. In many cases, the consequences of ineffective practices lead to restructuring, elimination of processes, and sometimes the displacement of training and performance improvement staff members. By implementing a sound ROI methodology, organizations can weed out ineffective programs or make existing programs more effective.

## Linking to Strategic Initiatives

The need to link processes to the strategic direction of the company applies to all functions—including training and performance improvement. The importance of linking programs to organizational strategy is another major reason to pursue a comprehensive measurement and evaluation process (Foshay 1998). Management often scrutinizes programs to determine what value they bring to the overall strategy. How do they fit? How will they help the organization achieve its goal? Are the "right" programs being offered, and if so, how do we know? The scenario in Exhibit 1 brings this issue to bear. The scenario represents a typical conversation between many training and performance improvement managers and executives, often to the demise of the training function. The need to link training and performance improvement programs to the organization's strategic objectives and report results that reflect these objectives bring a greater interest in the accountability of such programs and drive the need for ROI.

## EXHIBIT 1

## GLOBAL COMMUNICATIONS

Sydney Mitchell has been serving as CEO for Global Communications for the past nine months. Sydney has a reputation of being aggressive in meeting goals, yet pragmatic and fair. Before making significant changes in Global Communications' organizational structure, Sydney has given each function one year to make strides toward meeting strategic objectives. These strategic objectives focus on increasing profits, market share, customer satisfaction ratings, and employee satisfaction ratings. She has clearly communicated these objectives throughout her first nine months and even holds monthly learning sessions with employees to help them understand the meaning and importance of each objective.

With three months remaining in the year, Sydney has been meeting with executives of each function for status reports. Today she is meeting with Donald Hodges, the president of the GlobalCom University, Global Communications' corporate university.

Donald Hodges was handpicked by the past CEO and believes the university is making a difference. He always receives rave reviews from participants after each program. Donald is ready for Sydney. He has a very flashy presentation and the results of all of his program evaluations are ready for review.

Sydney: Hi Donald. The place looks great and everyone seems really busy.

Donald: Yes, Sydney. We're developing twelve new programs.

Sydney: Really. What are these programs?

Donald: Well, we're developing a new communications program. We're also revising our orientation program to include our new benefits package. We've also had requests from employees to offer programs they're interested in including a Dress for Success program, a time management program, and a business etiquette program. And we're developing a leadership program similar to one I attended recently.

Sydney: Hmmmm. How much time does it take to develop these programs?

Donald: Oh, not long. About a week for each day of training at the most. We have each of our four program developers working on three each. So I estimate it will take a few months to develop all twelve programs.

Sydney: I see. A few months...

Donald: Come on in the conference room, Sydney. I want to share with you our accomplishments thus far!

Donald "boots up" the presentation. He goes through all the preliminary issues, then gets to the results of the past nine months.

Donald: In the past nine months we have developed ten new programs, offered 1,120 hours of training, had 1,500 employees attend training, and received on average 4.5 out of 5 on the program satisfaction rating. So basically, we have developed new training, offered some new programs as well as some old favorites, and the employees attending training seem to think we're moving in the right direction.

Sydney: Do we know about the success of these programs on the job?

Donald: Not specifically, but we are confident that they are adding value.

Sydney: How do you know you're adding value?

Donald: Because of the feedback we receive.

Sydney: What kind of feedback do you receive?

Donald: Many of the participants tell us how successful they've been with what they have learned.

Sydney: So, you've actually had a follow-up of each program?

Donald: No, not exactly. We just receive random comments.

Sydney: So you have no organized way of knowing about the success of your programs?

Donald: Well, it's not a formal follow-up, but we still receive good feedback.

Sydney: I see. Well, thanks, Donald. I'd like to meet with you next Monday to discuss your activities further.

> ➤ You're Donald. How do you think the meeting went?
> ➤ You're Sydney. How do you think the meeting went?
> ➤ What is the fate of GlobalCom University?

## Top Executive Requirements

Increased interest in ROI from the executive suite is becoming commonplace in organizations in the US as well as other countries around the world. Top executives who have watched their training and performance improvement budgets grow without the appropriate accountability measures are becoming frustrated, and, in an attempt to respond to the situation, they are demanding a return on investment for these programs. Executives have to make appropriate funding decisions based on the impact programs bring to the financial health of their organizations. Without a measure that can be compared across all programs and processes, the decisions are often based on perception or political interest. Training and performance improvement managers and staff must show evidence of program impact using a measure that is compatible with those used in other operational elements so that top executives can operate the organization effectively.

## Growth in Training and Performance Improvement Budgets

As reported by *Training*'s annual industry report (2001), 1991 through 2001 saw a steady increase in US training budgets (see figure 1.1). Training budgets saw a 5 percent increase over 2000. This increase in training budgets and the actual expenditures reflected by these numbers can make the training and performance improvement function a target for criticism, bringing an increased need for accountability, including ROI. Further, it has been estimated that only 50 percent of all training content is still being used by employees one year after program delivery (Broad and Newstrom 1992). Considering the $56.8 billion spent on training in 2001, this represents a loss of $28.4 billion to organizations for training not fully used on the job.

## The Need for Balanced Measures

There is continuous debate as to what should or should not be measured and which results provide the best evidence of training impact. Some prefer soft measures obtained directly from clients and consumers such as work habits, work climate, and attitudes. Others prefer hard data focused on key issues of output, quality, cost, and time. A better system employs a balanced set of measures that takes into consideration participant preferences, learning, application, change in business measures, and actual ROI, as well as intangible measures. Data should be examined from a variety of sources, at different time periods, and for different purposes. The need for balanced measures is a major driver

**FIGURE 1.1**

## GROWTH IN TRAINING BUDGETS

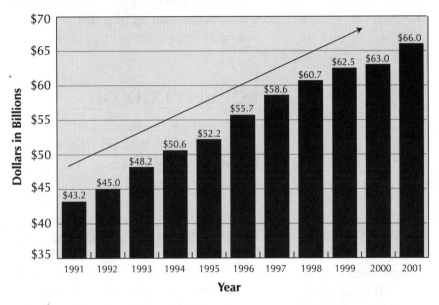

Sources: *Training*. 2000. Industry Report 2000. *Training* 37, no. 10 (October): 45-48. *Training*. 2001. Industry Report 2001. *Training* 38, no. 10 (October): 42-48.

Note: For comparative purposes, the 1991–2001 figures assume hardware and facilities expenses (excluded from *Training*'s baselines for 2000 and 2001). This table assumes hardware and facilities expenses of $9 billion for 2000 and 2001, the amount allocated in *Training*'s 1999 report.

of the ROI methodology in that it provides financial impact (ROI) along with the other important measures.

## Desire to Contribute

Individuals engaged in professional work want to know their efforts make a difference. Training and performance improvement staff members are no different. They need to see they are making a contribution in terms managers and executives respect and appreciate. One of the most self-satisfying parts of training and performance improvement may be showing the ROI of key programs. A comprehensive measurement and evaluation process not only shows the success of a program in terms of schedule, budget, and client feedback, but also reflects the actual monetary value added. An impressive ROI provides the final touch to a major program. This type of evaluation serves as evidence for staff, training managers, or senior management that training and performance improvement programs do make a difference.

## BENEFITS OF THE ROI METHODOLOGY

Although the benefits of adopting a comprehensive measurement and evaluation process including ROI may seem obvious, routine use of the ROI methodology can generate several specific benefits. Collectively, these benefits add enough value to develop a positive ROI on implementing ROI.

### Show the Contribution of Selected Programs

With ROI, both the client and the training and performance improvement staff will know the specific contribution of a program. The ROI calculation will show the actual net benefits versus the cost, elevating the evaluation data to a clear level of accountability. This process presents indisputable evidence of program success. When a program succeeds, in many cases the same type of program can be applied to other areas in the organization. Thus, if one division has success with a program and another division has the same needs, the program may add the same value to that division, enhancing the overall success of all training and performance improvement programs.

### Earn the Respect of Senior Management

Demonstrating the impact of training and performance improvement programs is one of the most convincing ways to earn the respect and support of the senior management team—and not just for one particular program. Managers respect processes and programs that add bottomline value in terms they understand. The result of ROI evaluation is comprehensive; when applied consistently to several programs, it can convince management that the training and performance improvement function is an important investment, not just an expense. Middle-level managers will see that training and performance improvement programs are making a viable contribution to their immediate objectives. ROI is a critical step toward helping the training and performance improvement department build a successful partnership with the senior management team.

## Gain the Confidence of Clients

The client, who requests and authorizes a program, will have a complete set of data to show the overall success of a program. Not hampered by a lack of qualitative or quantitative data, the balanced profile of results from the ROI methodology provides coverage from different sources, at different time frames, and with different types of data. Implementing the ROI methodology provides the information needed to validate the initial decision to move forward with a new program, continue an existing program, or eliminate an ineffective program.

## Improve Training and Performance Improvement Processes

Because a variety of feedback data are collected during the evaluation of a training program, the comprehensive analysis provides data to drive changes in training and performance improvement processes and makes adjustments during program implementation. It also provides data that help improve future programs by identifying which processes are nonproductive and which add value. Thus, ROI evaluation becomes an important process improvement tool both during and after the training program.

## Develop a Results-Based Approach

The entire process of ROI evaluation requires that all stakeholders be involved, including program designers and developers, facilitators, and evaluators. Throughout the training program design and implementation cycle, the entire team of stakeholders focuses on results. From detailed planning to the actual communication of results, every team member has a responsibility to achieve success. This focus often enhances the evaluation results because the ultimate outcomes are clearly in mind. In essence, the program begins with the end in mind. All the processes, activities, and steps focus on evaluation measures, from how well participants respond to the program to the actual ROI. As the function demonstrates success, confidence grows, enhancing results of future program evaluations.

## Alter or Eliminate Ineffective Programs

If a training or performance improvement program is not going well and results are not materializing, the data from ROI will prompt changes or modifications to the program. These changes can take place during program implementation so that the final results are positive. Or changes can take place in between program offerings based on the results of the comprehensive evaluation. By staying on track with the evaluation process, programs can continuously evolve so as to enhance overall results. On the other hand, a comprehensive ROI evaluation can provide evidence the program will not achieve desired results. While it takes courage to eliminate a program, in the long term, this action will reap important benefits.

## ROI on the ROI

Most training organizations spend less than 1 percent of their direct budgets on measurement and evaluation processes. This figure only considers the post-program analysis or comprehensive review process. Interjecting accountability throughout a program requires expenditures closer to 4 to 5 percent of the total training and performance improvement budget. Use of the ROI methodology will generate specific measurable savings to offset this expenditure. Among these are:

➤ Preventing unnecessary programs (after an evaluation of a pilot indicates that it will not add value);

➤ Altering or redesigning existing programs to make them more effective (and less expensive);

➤ Eliminating unproductive and ineffective programs (and saving the costs);

➤ Expanding the implementation of successful programs (adding value to other divisions, regions, etc.).

Many organizations keep a running total of the monetary benefits derived from implementing an ROI methodology. In comparing these benefits to the cost of implementation, the results yield a significant "ROI on the ROI."

## CHAPTER 2

# Who Should Use ROI

*A*ccountability *in training and performance improvement* does not apply to just one particular type of organization. Bringing accountability to programs or processes is a basic concern for organizations regardless of their product, service, mission, or scope. Accountability issues exist in organizations during favorable as well as unfavorable economic times. In good economic times, expenditures increase and organizational leaders are concerned that investments are properly allocated. In tough economic times, programs and processes that yield the best results are most likely to survive reorganization and restructuring efforts. A comprehensive evaluation can often help pinpoint the areas in which to place available funding.

Table 2.1 provides a profile of some of *Training*'s top 50 training organizations currently using or pursuing comprehensive measurement and evaluation processes including ROI (Galvin 2001). While the profile represents private sector organizations, public sector organizations are quickly adapting ROI to measure the impact of their programs (Phillips 2002). For decades the public sector relied on cost-benefit analysis to evaluate the use of resources (Nas 1996). But while cost-benefit analysis

**TABLE 2.1**

## ORGANIZATIONS USING COMPREHENSIVE EVALUATION INCLUDING ROI

| Company Name | Annual Training Budget | Training's Percent of Budget | Training Hours Per Employee | Percent On-the-Job Skills | Percent Personal Development |
|---|---|---|---|---|---|
| IBM | $1b | N/A | 60 | 80% | 20% |
| Synovus | $10m | 1.3% | 40-60 | 70% | 30% |
| AllState | $73.3m | 1.6% | 46 | 35% | 65% |
| Kinko's | $30m | 6% | 80 | 80% | 20% |
| Solectron Corp. | $10m (CA only) | N/A | 40 (CA only) | 67% | 33% |
| A.G. Edwards & Sons | $17.45m | 1.42% | 15.6 | 77% | 23% |

Adapted from: *Galvin T.* 2001. Birds of a feather. *Training* 38, no. 3 (March): 70-77.

takes into account similar measures as the actual ROI calculation (Thompson 1980), it falls short of the balanced approach of the ROI methodology (as discussed in chapter 1). Therefore, public sector organizations are also moving towards use of the ROI methodology to report all of the measures that explain the impact of training and performance improvement programs.

## THE TYPICAL ORGANIZATION

While the ROI methodology is suitable for any organization, the organizations currently implementing ROI as part of their training and performance improvement evaluation process share some similar characteristics. Typical characteristics include:

**Size of the organization.** Currently, the typical organizations that are implementing ROI are large. Whether in the public or private sector, large organizations tend to deliver a variety of programs to a diverse target audience—usually throughout a vast geographical area. Organizations delivering a variety of programs usually have some programs they could do without, and it is important to ensure they are offering the right programs at the right time to the right people. Large organizations also have the budget to develop comprehensive evaluation approaches. However, ROI *should* be built in the accountability process in smaller organizations as well. Small organizations have an even greater reason to conserve resources and ensure they're getting the most out of their dollar. Using several cost-saving approaches described later, small organizations (and larger organizations with limited budgets) can implement ROI with credible results.

**Size and visibility of the training and performance improvement budget.** The budget is usually large and has the attention of the senior management team. As shown in table 2.1, IBM has a training budget of $1 billion, an enormous budget by most companies' standards. Kinko's budget of $30 million, while a good deal smaller than IBM's, is 6 percent of the total payroll—a high percentage of payroll in comparison to some organizations. Edward Jones (not shown on this table) designates 13 percent of payroll to training (Galvin 2001). Regardless of how it is measured, whether as total budget, expenditure per employee, percentage of payroll, or percentage of revenue, a large training and performance improvement budget brings appropriate focus to additional measurement and evaluation. Executives will demand increased accountability for large expenditures.

**Focus on measurement.** Typically, organizations implementing ROI focus on establishing a variety of measures throughout the organization. Organizations already using well-known processes such as the Balanced Scorecard, Economic Value Added (EVA), Six Sigma, and others are ideal candidates for the ROI methodology because they already have a measurement-focused environment.

**Key drivers requiring additional accountability.** The presence of the drivers discussed in chapter 1 brings additional focus to accountability. These drivers create the need to change current practices. In most situations, multiple drivers create interest in ROI accountability.

**Level of change taking place.** Organizations using ROI are usually undergoing significant change. As an organization adjusts to competitive pressures, it is transforming, restructuring, and reorganizing. Significant change often increases interest in bottomline issues, resulting in a need for greater accountability.

## SYMPTOMS THAT THE ORGANIZATION IS READY FOR ROI

Several revealing symptoms indicate that an organization is ready to implement ROI for training and performance improvement programs. Many of these symptoms reflect the key drivers discussed in chapter 1 which cause pressure to pursue ROI.

1.  **Pressure from senior management to measure results**. This pressure can be a direct requirement to measure program effectiveness or a subtle expression of concern about the accountability of training and performance improvement programs.

2.  **Extremely low current investments in measurement and evaluation.** As indicated earlier, most organizations spend about 1 percent of their direct training and performance improvement budget on measurement and evaluation processes. Investments significantly lower than this amount may indicate there is little, if any, measurement and evaluation taking place, signalling the need for greater accountability. Expenditures in the 4 to 5 percent range indicate that training and performance improvement are already undergoing serious evaluation.

3. **Recent disasters with training and performance improvement programs.** Every organization has had one or more situations where a major program was implemented with no success. When there are multiple program failures, the training and performance improvement function often bears direct responsibility—or at least blame. These failures may prompt the implementation of measurement and evaluation processes to determine the impact of training and performance improvement programs, or more appropriately, to forecast ROI prior to implementation.

4. **A new director or leader in the training and performance improvement function.** A new leader often serves as a catalyst to change and may initiate a review process of previous programs' success rates. These individuals do not have the stigma of ownership or attachment to old programs and are willing to take an objective view. However, the desire to gain an immediate gauge of program effectiveness may lead to impatience if an evaluation process is not already in place.

5. **Managers' desire to build cutting-edge training and performance improvement functions.** Some managers strive to build cutting-edge training and performance improvement functions. In doing so, they may automatically build comprehensive measurement and evaluation processes into the overall strategy. These managers often set the pace for measurement and evaluation by highlighting the fact that they are serious about bringing accountability to their function. These functions have formal guidelines around their measurement process and build evaluation into the program development. They often begin with a thorough needs assessment to determine the best solution, then monitor the progress of the program and determine the business impact.

6. **Lack of management support for the training and performance improvement effort.** In some cases, the image of the training and performance improvement function suffers to the point that management no longer supports its efforts. While the unsatisfactory image may be caused by a number of factors, increased accountability often focuses on improving systems and processes, thereby shoring up the department's image.

Table 2.2 (also in appendix 1) provides a self-check to determine an organization's candidacy for ROI implementation.

## TABLE 2.2

### IS YOUR ORGANIZATION A CANDIDATE FOR ROI IMPLEMENTATION?

Read each question and check off the most appropriate level of agreement on a scale of 1 to 5 (1 = Total Disagreement; 5 = Total Agreement).

| | | Disagree | | | Agree | |
|---|---|---|---|---|---|---|
| | | 1 | 2 | 3 | 4 | 5 |
| 1. | My organization is considered a large organization with a wide variety of training and performance improvement programs. | ❑ | ❑ | ❑ | ❑ | ❑ |
| 2. | We have a large training and performance improvement budget that reflects the interest of senior management. | ❑ | ❑ | ❑ | ❑ | ❑ |
| 3. | Our organization has a culture of measurement and is focused on establishing a variety of measures including training and performance improvement. | ❑ | ❑ | ❑ | ❑ | ❑ |
| 4. | My organization is undergoing significant change. | ❑ | ❑ | ❑ | ❑ | ❑ |
| 5. | There is pressure from senior management to measure results of our training and performance improvement programs. | ❑ | ❑ | ❑ | ❑ | ❑ |
| 6. | My training and performance improvement function currently has a very low investment in measurement and evaluation. | ❑ | ❑ | ❑ | ❑ | ❑ |
| 7. | My organization has experienced more than one program disaster in the past. | ❑ | ❑ | ❑ | ❑ | ❑ |
| 8. | My organization has a new training and performance improvement leader. | ❑ | ❑ | ❑ | ❑ | ❑ |
| 9. | My team would like to be the leaders in training and performance improvement processes. | ❑ | ❑ | ❑ | ❑ | ❑ |
| 10. | The image of our training and performance improvement function is less than satisfactory. | ❑ | ❑ | ❑ | ❑ | ❑ |

## TABLE 2.2

## IS YOUR ORGANIZATION A CANDIDATE FOR ROI IMPLEMENTATION?

| | Disagree | | | Agree | |
|---|---|---|---|---|---|
| | 1 | 2 | 3 | 4 | 5 |
| 11. My clients are demanding that our training and performance improvement processes show bottom-line results. | ❏ | ❏ | ❏ | ❏ | ❏ |
| 12. My training and performance improvement function competes with other functions within our organization for resources. | ❏ | ❏ | ❏ | ❏ | ❏ |
| 13. There is increased focus on linking training and performance improvement processes to the strategic direction of the organization. | ❏ | ❏ | ❏ | ❏ | ❏ |
| 14. My training and performance improvement function is a key player in change initiatives currently taking place in my organization. | ❏ | ❏ | ❏ | ❏ | ❏ |
| 15. Our overall training and performance improvement budget is growing, and we are required to prove the bottom-line value of our processes. | ❏ | ❏ | ❏ | ❏ | ❏ |

## SCORING

If you scored:

**15–30** You are not yet a candidate for ROI.

**31–45** You are not a strong candidate for ROI. However, it is time to start pursuing some type of measurement process.

**46–60** You are a candidate for building skills to implement the ROI methodology. At this point there is no real pressure to show the ROI, which is the best time to perfect the process within the organization.

**61–75** You should already be implementing a comprehensive measurement and evaluation process including ROI.

Adapted from: Phillips, Jack J., Ron Stone, and Patricia P. Phillips. 2001. *The Human Resources Scorecard: Measuring the Return on Investment.* Boston: Butterworth-Heinemann.

## CHAPTER 3

# Building a Credible Process: The Evaluation Puzzle

**D**eveloping a credible and comprehensive *measurement and evaluation process* is much like putting together the pieces of a puzzle. The Evaluation Puzzle in figure 3.1 represents all of these major elements.

The first piece of the puzzle is the *evaluation framework*. This framework defines the levels at which programs are evaluated and how data are captured at different times from different sources. The second piece of the puzzle is the *ROI model*. An ROI model is critical in that it depicts the systematic steps to ensure consistent application of the evaluation methodology. The third piece of the evaluation puzzle is *operating standards and guidelines*. These standards build credibility in the process by supporting a systematic methodology and conservative approach to ROI evaluation. The standards and guidelines also support consistency in the process. The fourth piece of the evaluation puzzle is *case applications and practices*. Case studies showing real world applications of the process provide support for implementation. The

## FIGURE 3.1

### THE EVALUATION PUZZLE

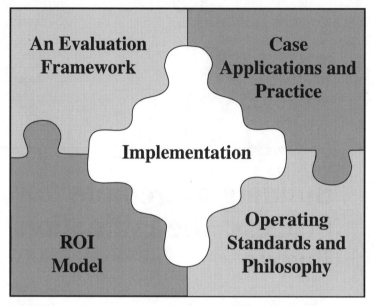

Adapted from: Phillips, Jack J. 2001. *The Consultant's Scorecard: Tracking Results and Bottom-Line Impact of Consulting Projects.* New York: McGraw-Hill.

final piece of the puzzle, *implementation,* brings together the other four pieces to implement the ROI methodology. Critical elements of implementation, which will be discussed later, ensure that the evaluation process is fully integrated into the organization; that the organization develops the appropriate skills, procedures, and guidelines; and that a comprehensive communication strategy is in place to ensure the process is utilized to its fullest while maintaining credibility with key stakeholders.

Together, these five pieces of the evaluation puzzle form a comprehensive measurement and evaluation system that contains a balanced set of measures, has credibility, and can be replicated from one group to another. The remainder of this book explains in detail the various pieces of the evaluation puzzle, with a focus on the ROI model.

## THE EVALUATION FRAMEWORK

The first piece of the evaluation puzzle is the evaluation framework. An important contribution to the field of training measurement and evaluation is the work of Donald Kirkpatrick. In the 1950s, Kirkpatrick developed a framework of four levels of evaluation (table 3.1).

### TABLE 3.1

### KIRKPATRICK'S FOUR LEVELS OF EVALUATION

| Level | Brief Description |
|---|---|
| 1. Reaction | Measures participants' reaction to the program |
| 2. Learning | Measures the extent to which participants change attitudes, improve knowledge, and/or increase skills |
| 3. Behavior | Measures the extent to which change in behavior occurs |
| 4. Results | Measures the changes in business results |

The first of Kirkpatrick's four levels is Reaction, a measure of participant reaction to the training program. Level 2, Learning, is the measure of changes in participant attitudes, knowledge, or skills as a result of the program. Kirkpatrick defines Level 3, Behavior, as the measure of change in behavior on the job after attending the program. Kirkpatrick's fourth level, Results, measures changes in business results such as productivity, quality, costs, sales, turnover, and higher profits (Kirkpatrick 1994).

Kirkpatrick's work provides the initial framework for evaluating training and performance improvement programs. However, the need to take evaluation a step further has intensified in the past decade. Increasingly, executives require the training and performance improvement function to show the value it brings to the organization in the same terms as other operational functions. The most common measure for value-added benefits in other operational functions is return on investment (Hornegren 1982; Anthony and Reece 1983). The ROI is the ratio of earnings (net benefits) to investment (costs) (Kearsley 1982).

In order to address training's need to show its financial contribution to the organization while balancing that data with the additional measures, Jack Phillips expands Kirkpatrick's four levels to add a fifth level, ROI (Phillips 1995). Table 3.2 illustrates Phillips' five-level evaluation framework.

This additional level of measurement takes into account the steps of the cost-benefit analysis process and the calculation of the ROI ratio. Where Kirkpatrick's fourth level stops at identifying the benefits of the program (Level 4, Results), Phillips converts the benefits to monetary value and compares the monetary benefit to the fully loaded costs of the program (Phillips 1996b). To ensure accuracy in calculating the return on investment, Phillips also includes a critical step, isolating the effects of the program (Phillips 1996a). Isolating the effects ensures an accurate picture of the program's benefits. Some insist that if it's not possible to use a scientific control group methodology to isolate the effects, this step will not be valid and should not be taken (Benson and Tran 2002). However, other appropriate methodologies are available,

## TABLE 3.2

### PHILLIPS' FIVE LEVELS OF EVALUATION

| Level | Brief Description |
|---|---|
| 1. Reaction, Satisfaction, and Planned Action | Measures participants' reaction to the program and stakeholder satisfaction with the program and the planned implementation |
| 2. Learning | Measures skills, knowledge, or attitude changes related to the program and implementation |
| 3. Application and Implementation | Measures changes in behavior on the job and specific application and implementation of the program |
| 4. Business Impact | Measures business impact changes related to the program |
| 5. Return on Investment | Compares the monetary value of the business impact with the costs for the program |

as will be discussed later in the book. Excluding this step entirely results in an incorrect, invalid, and inappropriate ROI calculation.

Table 3.3 provides a comparison of Kirkpatrick's framework, Phillips' framework, and the cost-benefit analysis process. As shown in table 3.3, both Kirkpatrick and Phillips address participant reaction as well as learning and application of skills or behavior change. Level 4 (Impact/Results) is comparable to the identification of benefits in cost-benefit analysis. Level 5, ROI, compares the benefits and the costs, as well as accounting for other influences.

Although this distinction between the frameworks is important, it is necessary to understand that not all programs are evaluated at all five levels. Perhaps the best explanation for this is that as the level of

## TABLE 3.3

### EVALUATION FRAMEWORKS COMPARED TO COST-BENEFIT ANALYSIS

| | Kirkpatrick's Four Levels | Phillips' Five Levels | CBA |
|---|:---:|:---:|:---:|
| Measure Participant Reaction | ✓ | ✓ | |
| Measure Learning | ✓ | ✓ | |
| Measure Application/ Behavior | ✓ | ✓ | |
| Measure Impact/Results/ Benefits | ✓ | ✓ | ✓ |
| Measure ROI | | ✓ | ✓ |
| Isolate the Effects of the Program | | ✓ | |
| Determine Cost | | ✓ | ✓ |
| Convert Benefits to Monetary Value | | ✓ | ✓ |
| Identify Intangible Benefits | ✓ | ✓ | ✓ |

evaluation increases, so does its difficulty and expense. It takes time and resources to do a comprehensive ROI study, so it's just not feasible to do it for every training program. Table 3.4 suggests some targets for evaluating training and performance improvement programs at the different levels.

Some programs are evaluated just for reaction, some just for learning, etc. Programs are selected for evaluation using criteria such as:

➤ Expected program life cycle;

➤ Importance of program in meeting the organization's goals;

➤ Cost of the program;

➤ Visibility of the program;

➤ Size of the target audience; and

➤ Extent of management interest.

However, when evaluating at a higher level, it is important to evaluate at lower levels as well. A chain of impact should occur through the levels of evaluation as participants react and plan action (Level 1) based on the skills and knowledge acquired during the program (Level 2) which are then applied on the job (Level 3), and the resulting business impact (Level 4). If measurements are not taken at each of these levels, it is difficult to conclude that the results achieved are actually a result of the training and performance improvement program. Because of

## TABLE 3.4

### SUGGESTED EVALUATION TARGETS

| Evaluation Levels | Measures | Percent |
|-------------------|----------|---------|
| Level 1 | Reaction, Satisfaction | 100% |
| Level 2 | Learning | 70% |
| Level 3 | Application | 30% |
| Level 4 | Impact | 20% |
| Level 5 | ROI | 5-10% |

this, evaluation should be conducted at all levels when an ROI evaluation is planned.

## THE ROI MODEL

The second piece of the evaluation puzzle is the ROI model. The ROI model shows the systematic steps to ensure the evaluation methodology is implemented consistently. Replication of the evaluation process is imperative. A step-by-step model will ensure the methodology can be used consistently. Figure 3.2 shows the ROI methodology model. The ROI model consists of four stages: Evaluation Planning, Data Collection, Data Analysis, and Communicate Results. The model will be explored in detail in the next two chapters.

## THE OPERATING STANDARDS: GUIDING PRINCIPLES

Operating standards, the third piece of the evaluation puzzle, help ensure that there is consistency in the evaluation process and that a conservative approach is taken. Standards and guiding principles keep the evaluation credible and allow for the replication of the process. When implementing ROI, there are ten guiding principles to use as operating standards (Phillips 1997a).

### 1. Report the Complete Story

*When conducting a higher level of evaluation, data must be collected at lower levels.* ROI is a critical measure, but it is only one of five measures necessary to explain the full impact of the program. So, lower levels of data must be included in the analysis. The data at the lower levels also provide important information that can be helpful in making adjustments for future program implementation.

### 2. Conserve Important Resources

*When an evaluation is planned for a higher level, the previous level of evaluation does not have to be comprehensive.* Lower level measures are critical in telling the complete story, and cannot be omitted. However,

# FIGURE 3.2
## ROI METHODOLOGY MODEL

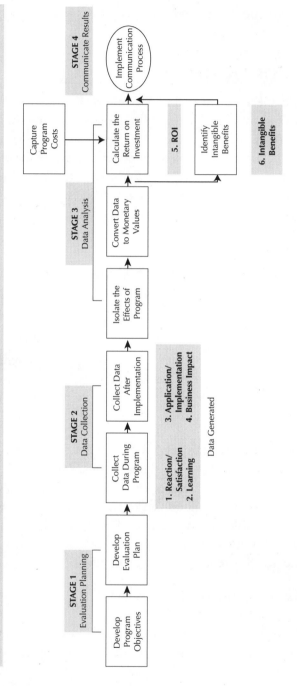

Adapted from: Phillips, Jack J., Ron Stone, and Patricia P. Phillips. 2001. *The Human Resources Scorecard: Measuring the Return on Investment*. Boston: Butterworth-Heinemann.

short-cuts *can* be taken to conserve resources. For example, when the client is interested in business impact, short-cuts can be taken at Levels 2 and 3.

## 3. Enhance Credibility

*When collecting and analyzing data, use only the most credible source.* Credibility is the most important factor in the measurement and evaluation process. Without it, the results are meaningless. Using the most credible source (often the participants) will enhance the perception of the quality and accuracy of data analysis and results.

## 4. Be Conservative

*When analyzing data, select the most conservative alternative for calculations.* This principle is at the heart of the evaluation process. A conservative approach lowers the ROI and helps build the needed credibility with the target audience. It's always better to be conservative than to provide a generous estimate and have results that are not credible.

## 5. Account for Other Factors

*At least one method must be used to isolate the effects of the program.* This step is imperative. Without some method to isolate the effects of the program, the evaluation results are considered highly inaccurate and overstated.

## 6. Account for Missing Data

*If no improvement data are available for a participant, assume that little or no improvement occurred.* If participants do not provide data— if they are no longer a part of the organization or they perform a different function—assume that little or no improvement has occurred. It damages the credibility of the evaluation to make assumptions about improvements you cannot be sure of. This ultra-conservative approach further enhances the credibility of the results.

## 7. Adjust Estimates for Error

*Adjust estimates of improvement for the potential error of the estimate.* This guideline contributes to the conservative approach of the process. Using estimates is very common in reporting financial and cost-benefit information. To enhance the credibility of estimated data used in ROI evaluation of training and performance improvement programs, estimates are weighted with a level of confidence, adjusting the estimate for potential error.

## 8. Omit the Extremes

*Extreme data items and unsupported claims should not be used in ROI calculations.* Again, to maintain credibility of results, steps should be taken to be conservative in the analysis. For example, if you have a list of numbers all ranging from 30 to 70 and one 100, that 100 would be considered an outlier or extreme data item. Extreme data items can skew results—both to the low side as well as the high side. In order to eliminate the influence of extreme data items, omit them from the analysis.

## 9. Capture Annual Benefits for Short-Term Programs

*Only the first year of benefits (annual) should be used in the ROI analysis of short-term programs.* If benefits are not quickly realized for most training and performance improvement programs, they are probably not worth the cost. Therefore, for short-term programs, consider only annual benefits. For more extensive programs, where implementation spans a year or more, then multiple year benefits are captured.

## 10. Isolate All Program Costs

*Program costs should be fully-loaded for ROI analysis.* All costs of the program are tabulated, beginning with the cost of the needs analysis and ending with the cost of the evaluation. As part of the conservative approach, the costs are loaded to reduce the ROI.

Collectively, these guiding principles ensure that the approach is conservative and that the impact study can be replicated, making them a crucial part of the puzzle. They also ensure that the ROI for training and performance improvement programs can be compared to the ROI of operational processes and initiatives in the organization.

## CASE APPLICATION AND PRACTICES

A critical piece of the evaluation puzzle is the development of case studies by the training and performance improvement function to show success, promote programs, or to justify new programs. Case studies from other organizations can also be used for benchmarking or as examples of success. Table 3.5 provides a sample of case studies published by the American Society for Training and Development (Phillips, Jack 1994, 1997c; Phillips, Patricia 2001). Case studies within similar industries indicate the status of ROI implementation in similar organizations—addressing similar issues and targeting similar concerns. Case studies from a global perspective provide evidence of success with the ROI methodology in a variety of organizations and industries, supporting the need to pursue comprehensive measurement and evaluation. Case studies also provide support to practitioners, managers, and executives interested in learning about how to apply the ROI methodology.

The use of case studies from other organizations is helpful in understanding the merits of ROI implementation and the success of specific programs. Studies developed by the organization, however, are more powerful in displaying evidence of success using the ROI methodology to evaluate internal programs.

## IMPLEMENTATION

The final piece of the evaluation puzzle is implementation. The best tool, technique, or model will not be successful unless it is properly utilized and becomes a routine part of the training and performance improvement function (Phillips 1997b). As with any change, the people affected by the implementation of a comprehensive measurement and evaluation process—in this case, the training staff and other stakeholders— will likely resist it. Some of that resistance will be based on realistic barriers. Part of it, however, will be based on

## TABLE 3.5

### ROI CASE STUDIES

| Organization | Industry | Program | ROI |
|---|---|---|---|
| Office of Personnel Management[1] | U.S. Government | Supervisory Training | 150% |
| Magnavox Electronic Systems Company[1] | Electronics | Literacy Training | 741% |
| Litton Guidance and Control Systems[1] | Avionics | Self-Directed Work Teams | 650% |
| Coca-Cola Bottling Company of San Antonio[1] | Soft Drinks | Supervisory Training | 1,447% |
| Commonwealth Edison[2] | Electrical Utility | Machine Operator | 57% |
| Texas Instruments[2] | Electronics | Sales Training Negotiation | 2,827% |
| Apple Computer[3] | Computer Manufacturing | Process Improvement | 182% |
| Hewlett-Packard Company[3] | Computer Support Services | Sales Training | 195% |
| First National Bank[3] | Financial Services | Sales Training | 555% |
| Nassau County Police Department[3] | Police Department | Interpersonal Skills Training | 144% |

Sources: [1]Phillips, Jack J., ed. 1994. *Measuring the Return On Investment Vol. 1.* Alexandria, VA: American Society for Training and Development.

[2]Phillips, Jack J., ed. 1998. *Measuring the Return On Investment Vol. 2.* Alexandria, VA: American Society for Training and Development.

[3]Phillips, Patricia P., ed. 2001. *Measuring the Return On Investment Vol. 3.* Alexandria, VA: American Society for Training and Development.

misunderstandings and perceived problems. In both cases, the organization must work to overcome the resistance by carefully and methodically implementing the ROI evaluation using the following critical steps:

1. Assign Responsibilities

2. Develop Skills

3. Develop an Implementation Plan

4. Prepare or Revise Evaluation Guidelines

5. Brief Managers on the Evaluation Process

## Assign Responsibilities

To ensure successful ROI implementation, assign responsibilities up-front—before implementation begins. Who will lead the evaluation effort? Will evaluation be integrated into the training function or will it report to the CFO? Is it more appropriate to contract with a third party evaluation provider and have only an internal coordinator? These questions and others must be considered when implementing any evaluation strategy.

## Develop Skills

Another key step in successful implementation is the development of skills and capabilities. A complete understanding of each step in the evaluation process will simplify implementation, reducing the stress and frustration often associated with jumping from one process to another.

## Develop an Implementation Plan

Planning for implementation will save time and money. By using a basic set of criteria to review existing programs as well as proposed new programs, the training function can develop an implementation plan. This plan will assist in determining which programs will be evaluated at which levels (by using the criteria discussed earlier) and how the necessary resources will be allocated.

Along with an implementation plan to select programs for different levels of evaluation, there should also be a project plan to help manage the overall evaluation process. From a practical standpoint, this project plan serves to support the transition from the present situation to a desired future situation. Table 3.6 provides a sample project plan.

This particular project plan includes ten steps to implementing the ROI methodology.

### TABLE 3.6

### PROJECT PLAN

| | Oct | Nov | Dec | Jan | Feb | Mar | Apr | May | Jun | Jul | Aug | Sep |
|---|---|---|---|---|---|---|---|---|---|---|---|---|
| 1. Review of Existing Programs, Processes, Reports, Data | ▓ | ▓ | | | | | | | | | | |
| 2. Skill Development | | | ▓ | | | | | | | | | |
| 3. Finalize Evaluation Planning Documents | | | ▓ | | | | | | | | | |
| 4. Evaluation Data Collection | | | | | ▓ | ▓ | | ▓ | | | | |
| 5. Analysis of Data | | | | | | | | | ▓ | | ▓ | |
| 6. Development of Reports | | | | | | | | | | ▓ | | |
| 7. Presentation of Impact Study Results | | | | | | | | | | | | ▓ |
| 8. Develop Scorecard Framework | | | | | | | | | ▓ | | ▓ | |
| 9. Develop Guidelines | | | | | ▓ | | ▓ | | ▓ | | | |
| 10. Manager Briefings | | | | | | | | | ▓ | | | |

1. **Review of existing programs, processes, reports, and data.** This step is essential in understanding past practices and how to incorporate the new methodology most effectively.

2. **Skill development.** Developing skills necessary to implement the ROI methodology is essential for complete integration into the training and performance improvement process.

3. **Finalize evaluation planning documents.** The planning documents necessary to implement the ROI methodology are critical in ensuring every step of the process is taken and that key stakeholders are in agreement with those steps.

4. **Evaluation data collection.** This step represents the data collection process.

5. **Analysis of the data.** This step represents the time necessary to analyze the data after collection.

6. **Development of reports.** As we will discuss in chapter 5, developing a variety of reports helps to address specific audience needs. A complete impact study will be developed for the training and performance improvement staff records. After the executive management understands the evaluation process, a brief summary (in some cases only a one-page summary) will be necessary.

7. **Presentation of impact study results.** Different audiences need different information. In the initial implementation of the ROI methodology, results should be presented in a formal setting to ensure clear communication of the process itself. Presentation of results to the staff members may take place in a less formal setting such as a weekly staff meeting.

8. **Develop scorecard framework.** In this particular example, the client requested a roll-up scorecard to report the results of all training and performance improvement programs.

9. **Develop guidelines.** As the methodology is implemented and integrated into the training and performance improvement function, guidelines are developed to ensure consistent and long-term implementation.

10. **Manager briefings.** Management understanding of the evaluation process is critical. Managers who are not involved in a particular evaluation project might still be interested in the process. Manager briefings are a way to not only communicate results of the evaluation but to communicate about the process in general.

Each individual program evaluation will have individual project plans to detail the steps necessary to complete the project as well as keep the evaluation project on track. Planning is the key to successful ROI implementation.

## Prepare or Revise Evaluation Guidelines

Guidelines keep the implementation process on track. A clear set of guidelines helps to ensure that the process continues as designed in the event of changes in staff or management. They also establish the evaluation process as an integral part of the overall training and performance improvement strategy.

## Brief Managers on the Evaluation Process

Communicating to managers about the evaluation process will help enlist their support during the implementation process. The unknown can often become a barrier, so if the organization makes the effort to explain each step, it's more likely managers as a whole will understand and support the evaluation efforts.

All five of the pieces of the evaluation puzzle are necessary to build a comprehensive measurement and evaluation process. The next two chapters take you through the ROI methodology step by step.

## CHAPTER 4

# The ROI Methodology

An effective ROI methodology must balance
many issues, including feasibility, simplicity, credibility, and soundness.
A methodology must balance all of these issues, in part, in order to
satisfy the needs and requirements of three major target audiences.
First, the training and performance improvement staff members who
use a process must have a clear, straight-forward approach. Otherwise,
the process may appear confusing and complex, causing many staff
members to assume that the ROI cannot be developed or that it is too
expensive for most applications. If staff members perceive the ROI
methodology as inconceivable, many will give up.

Second, an ROI methodology must meet the unique requirements
of the clients—those who request and approve programs. Clients need
a process that will provide quantitative and qualitative results. They
need a process that will develop a calculation similar to the ROI formula
applied to other types of investments and a process that reflects their
frame of reference, background, and level of understanding. More
importantly, they need a process with which they can identify—one
that is sound, realistic, and practical enough to earn their confidence.

Finally, the process needs the support of researchers. The process
must hold up under their scrutiny and close examination. Researchers

want to use models, formulas, assumptions, and theories that are sound and based on commonly accepted practices. Also, they want a process that produces accurate values and consistent outcomes. They want a process that can be replicated reliably from one situation to another. If two different practitioners are evaluating a program, the process should result in the same measurements.

## CRITERIA FOR AN EFFECTIVE ROI METHODOLOGY

An ROI methodology must meet certain criteria to meet the critical challenges of those who will be using it. The following criteria came out of working with training and performance improvement managers and specialists to develop comprehensive measurement and evaluation processes within their organizations.

### Simple

The ROI methodology must be simple—void of complex formulas, lengthy equations, and complicated methodologies. Most ROI models do not meet these criteria. In an attempt to obtain statistical perfection, many ROI models and processes are too complex to understand and use. Consequently, they are not implemented. While there is merit in striving for statistical accuracy, if a model is so complicated it can't be used, the organization doesn't stand to benefit much.

### Economical

The ROI methodology must be economical and easily implemented. While the initial implementation of any new methodology can be costly, once the methodology is integrated into the organization and has become a routine part of the training and performance improvement process, minimal additional resources will be required to sustain its implementation.

### Credible

The assumptions, methodology, and outcomes of the evaluation process must be credible. Logical, methodical steps earn the respect of practitioners, senior managers, and researchers. This requires not only a theoretically sound process, but a process that is very practical in its approach as well.

## Theoretically Sound

From a research perspective, the ROI methodology must be theoretically sound and based on generally accepted practices. Unfortunately, this requirement can lead to an extensive, complicated process. Ideally, the process must strike a balance between maintaining a practical, sensible approach and ensuring a sound and theoretical basis for the procedures. This is perhaps one of the greatest challenges to those who develop models for ROI measurement.

## Accounts for Other Factors

An ROI methodology must account for other factors that influence output measures targeted by the program. This is one of the most often overlooked issues, but is necessary to build credibility and accuracy within the process. The ROI methodology should pinpoint the program's contribution while considering all other influences.

## Appropriate

The ROI methodology should be appropriate for a variety of training and performance improvement programs. Some models apply to only a small number of programs, such as those focused on productivity improvement. Ideally, the process must be applicable to all types of training and performance improvement programs as well as other programs, such as career development, organizational development, and major change initiatives. It's not practical for the organization to need a different type of evaluation process for every type of program.

## Flexible

The ROI methodology must have the flexibility to be applied on a pre-program basis as well as a post-program basis. In some situations, an estimate of the ROI is required before developing the actual program. The process should be flexible enough to adjust to a range of potential time frames for calculating the ROI.

## Applicable

The ROI methodology must be applicable with both hard and soft data. Hard data is typically represented as output, quality, cost, and time. Soft data includes job satisfaction, customer satisfaction, absenteeism, turnover, grievances, and complaints.

## Considers All Costs

The ROI methodology must include all of the *fully-loaded* costs associated with the training and performance improvement programs. These costs include the initial needs assessment; development; delivery costs including facilitator, facility, and participant costs; and evaluation costs. Although the term ROI has been used loosely to express any of the benefits of a training and performance improvement program, an acceptable ROI methodology includes monetary costs. Omitting or understating costs will destroy the credibility of the ROI results.

## Successful Track Record

Finally, the ROI methodology needs a successful track record with a variety of types of applications. In far too many situations, models are created which may look good but are never applied successfully. An effective measurement and evaluation process should withstand the wear and tear of implementation and prove valuable to users.

These criteria are essential, and to be worthwhile for the organization, the ROI methodology should meet the vast majority, if not all, of the criteria. The bad news, however, is that most models do not meet these criteria. Table 4.1 provides a checklist you can use to evaluate some common established processes against the criteria.

## THE ROI METHODOLOGY

The ROI methodology model shown in figure 4.1(see the foldout on the last page) generates a scorecard of six types of data:

1. Reaction, satisfaction, and planned action

2. Learning

**TABLE 4.1**

**CRITERIA CHECKLIST**
**How Does Your Measurement and Evaluation Process Compare?**

| Criteria | ROI Methodology | Balanced Scorecard | Vital Signs | Economic Value Added | Other |
|---|---|---|---|---|---|
| Simple | ✓ | | | | |
| Economical | ✓ | | | | |
| Credible | ✓ | | | | |
| Theoretically sound | ✓ | | | | |
| Accounts for other factors | ✓ | | | | |
| Appropriate with a variety of programs | ✓ | | | | |
| Applicable on pre-program and post-program basis | ✓ | | | | |
| Measures hard data and soft data | ✓ | | | | |
| Includes all fully-loaded costs | ✓ | | | | |
| Successful track record | ✓ | | | | |

3. Application and implementation

4. Business impact

5. ROI

6. Intangible benefits

As shown in figure 4.1, the process also includes the critical step of isolating the effects of the program. This ROI methodology, developed by Jack Phillips, provides a balanced approach to evaluating training and performance improvement programs and meets all of the criteria for an effective methodology.

The process is divided into four stages. The first stage addresses *evaluation planning*. This critical step begins with the development of program objectives and comprehensive evaluation plans. The second stage represents the *data collection* process. Data are collected at different time frames and from different sources to develop a balanced set of measures. The third stage of the process is the *data analysis*. At this stage, the practitioners isolate the program from other influences, convert data to monetary value, tabulate program costs, and calculate the ROI. It is also at this stage that the intangible benefits, those benefits not converted to monetary value, are identified. The final stage of the process is the *communication of results*. While the last step in this comprehensive process, communication of results is one of the most critical and will be explored in detail in the next chapter.

## EVALUATION PLANNING

The first stage of the ROI methodology, evaluation planning, is one of the most critical. Thorough planning ensures that the evaluation addresses the appropriate objectives, utilizes the proper data collection instruments, and that the client agrees on data analysis methodologies. The evaluation planning stage includes two steps: developing program objectives and developing the evaluation plan.

### Develop Program Objectives

Before the ROI evaluation begins, the program objectives must be developed. The objectives form the basis for determining the depth of the evaluation, meaning that they determine what level of evaluation will take place. Program objectives range from participant reaction to the actual ROI calculation. Program objectives link directly to the results of the front-end analysis. As shown in figure 4.2, once the organization or function determines the business need, a thorough needs analysis identifies the performance necessary to meet that need. The skills and/ or knowledge needed to achieve the desired performance are identified, taking into consideration the participant preferences for learning. For

## FIGURE 4.1

## ROI METHODOLOGY MODEL

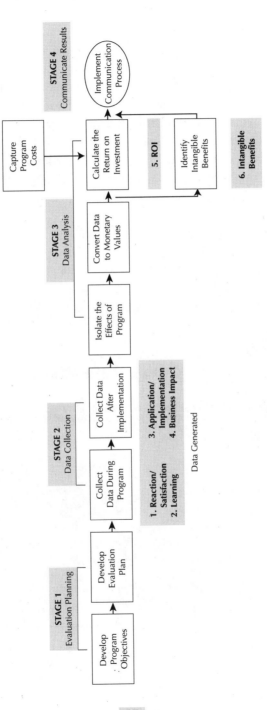

Adapted from: Phillips, Jack J., Ron Stone, and Patricia P. Phillips. 2001. *The Human Resources Scorecard: Measuring the Return on Investment.* Boston: Butterworth-Heinemann.

each of these discrepancies in skills and knowledge, it's necessary to develop objectives in order to ensure program success and link those objectives to levels of evaluation.

Participant satisfaction objectives link to Level 1 evaluation. Learning objectives link to Level 2 evaluation. Job performance objectives link to Level 3 evaluation, application. Business objectives link to Level 4, business impact evaluation. Finally the desired ROI from the program links to the ROI outcome of the evaluation process.

Table 4.2 provides a list of objectives that focus on the various levels of evaluation. Use the blank line at the end of each objective to test your understanding.

## Develop Evaluation Plan

After defining program objectives, the next step is to develop the evaluation plan. This plan is critical in ensuring that each step of the evaluation process is addressed appropriately. As shown in tables 4.3

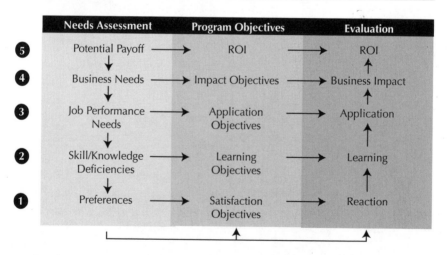

**FIGURE 4.2**

**LINKING NEEDS, OBJECTIVES, AND EVALUATION**

| Needs Assessment | Program Objectives | Evaluation |
|---|---|---|
| 5 Potential Payoff → | ROI → | ROI |
| 4 Business Needs → | Impact Objectives → | Business Impact |
| 3 Job Performance Needs → | Application Objectives → | Application |
| 2 Skill/Knowledge Deficiencies → | Learning Objectives → | Learning |
| 1 Preferences → | Satisfaction Objectives → | Reaction |

Adapted from: Phillips, Jack J., Ron Stone, and Patricia P. Phillips. 2001. *The Human Resources Scorecard: Measuring the Return on Investment.* Boston: Butterworth-Heinemann.

## TABLE 4.2

## MATCHING EVALUATION LEVELS WITH OBJECTIVES

Instructions: For each objective listed below, indicate the level of evaluation at which the objective is aimed.

**Level 1. Reaction, Satisfaction, and Planned Action**

**Level 2. Learning**

**Level 3. Application and Implementation**

**Level 4. Business Impact**

**Level 5. Return on Investment**

| Objective | Evaluation Level |
|---|---|
| 1. Decrease error rates on reports by 20%. | _____ |
| 2. Increase the use of disciplinary discussion skills in 90% of situations where work habits are unacceptable. | _____ |
| 3. Achieve a post-test score increase of 30% over pre-test. | _____ |
| 4. Initiate at least three cost reduction projects. | _____ |
| 5. Decrease the amount of time required to complete a project. | _____ |
| 6. Achieve a 2:1 benefit to cost ratio one year after program implementation. | _____ |
| 7. Receive an instructor rating from participants of at least 4.5 out of 5. | _____ |
| 8. Increase the external customer satisfaction index by 25% in 3 months. | _____ |
| 9. Handle customer complaints with the 5 step process in 95% of complaint situations. | _____ |
| 10. At least 50% of participants use all customer interaction skills with every customer. | _____ |

Answers: 1) L- 4; 2) L-3; 3) L-2; 4) L-3; 5) L-4; 6) L-5; 7) L-1; 8) L-4; 9) L-3; 10) L-3

Adapted from: Phillips, Jack J., and Ron Stone. 2001. *Measuring Training Success*. New York: McGraw-Hill.

and 4.4, the actual evaluation planning documents address each step of the process. The steps in the planning process include developing a detailed data collection plan as well as a plan to analyze the data. The data collection plan first includes broad program objectives. (The detailed objectives are developed in the previous step.) For planning purposes, only broad objectives are necessary. Next the practitioner defines the specific measures. Determining how to evaluate each objective upfront will save time and confusion later. The next steps include determining how to collect the data and from what sources to obtain it. Practitioners also determine the timing of the data collection during the initial planning stage, as well as who will be responsible for gathering the various data items from the different sources.

After developing the data collection plan, Level 4 data items are moved to the ROI analysis plan. In this second phase of the planning process, practitioners decide the methods for isolating the effects of the program and converting data to monetary value. Program costs

## TABLE 4.3

### DATA COLLECTION PLAN

Program: _____

Responsibility: _____ Date: _____

| Level | Broad Program Objectives | Measures/ Data | Data Collection Method | Data Source | Timing of Data Collection | Responsibilities for Data Collection |
|---|---|---|---|---|---|---|
| 1. Reaction and Planned Action | | | | | | |
| 2. Learning | | | | | | |
| 3. Application | | | | | | |
| 4. Impact | | | | | | |
| 5. ROI | | | | | | |

Source: Phillips, Jack J., and Patricia Pulliam. 1999. *Mastering ROI*. Alexandria, VA: American Society for Training and Development.

are identified as well as the Level 4 business measures that will not be converted to monetary value—the intangible benefits. Other potential influences that may affect the identified business measures are also noted during this phase. Finally, the practitioner identifies the target audiences to receive the final results.

Planning the evaluation is critical. Although much time and effort is put into this process, planning has many advantages.

➤ Planning provides a road map to complete the evaluation process.

➤ Agreeing upfront with the client how the evaluation will take place will save frustration (from both parties) during the process.

➤ Presenting the plan to the training staff, including facilitators, will communicate expectations of program success and the process by which success will be measured. This step reinforces to the staff that the evaluation is a process improvement tool, rather than an individual performance evaluation.

## TABLE 4.4

### ROI ANALYSIS PLAN

| Data Items | Methods of Isolating Effects of Program | Methods of Converting Data | Cost Categories | Intangible Benefits | Other Influences/ Issues | Communication Targets |
|---|---|---|---|---|---|---|
|  |  |  |  |  |  |  |

Source: Phillips, Jack J., and Patricia Pulliam. 1999. *Mastering ROI*. Alexandria, VA: American Society for Training and Development.

➤ Communicating the evaluation plan to program participants will reaffirm the importance of the program. It will also prepare participants to provide appropriate data at the appropriate time. This not only helps ensure credible data is received, but will also help increase response rates.

## DATA COLLECTION

The second stage of the ROI methodology is data collection. Data are collected at two time frames—during the training program and on a post-program basis. Data are collected during the program to measure participant reaction and satisfaction as well as learning. These measures help ensure that adjustments are made as needed to keep the program on track. The reaction, satisfaction, and learning data are critical for immediate feedback to make changes. Reaction data can also be useful in predicting application, as well as forecasting impact data and the ROI (Phillips 1997a; Alampay and Morgan 2000; APQC 2000).

Data are also collected on a post-program basis. Following the program, practitioners gather information regarding the application of skills and knowledge as well as the impact the program has had on the organizations. They collect both hard data and soft data using a variety of methods such as:

➤ Follow-up surveys to measure satisfaction from stakeholders;

➤ Follow-up questionnaires to measure reaction and uncover specific application issues;

➤ On-the-job observation to capture actual application and use;

➤ Tests and assessments to measure the extent of learning (knowledge gained or skills enhanced);

➤ Interviews to measure reaction and determine the extent to which the program has been implemented;

➤ Focus groups to determine the degree of application of new skills or knowledge on-the-job;

70

➤ Action plans to show progress with implementation on the job and the impact obtained;

➤ Performance contracts to detail specific outcomes expected or obtained from the program;

➤ Business performance monitoring to show improvement in various performance records and operational data.

The important challenge in data collection is selecting the method or methods appropriate for the setting and the specific program, within the time and budget constraints.

## DATA ANALYSIS

The third stage is data analysis. At this stage the results of the program begin to become clear. By isolating the effects of the training program, results are more accurate—there is minimal question as to how much of the results can actually be contributed to the program. Data conversion takes place so that program benefits can be converted to monetary value. The costs are tabulated and the ROI calculation is developed in this stage. Finally the intangible benefits are identified. Each of these steps is presented in greater detail below.

### Isolate the Effects of the Program

An often-overlooked issue in evaluating training and performance improvement programs is the process of isolating the effects of the program. There are several specific strategies that determine the amount of performance improvement directly related to the program. Isolating the effects is essential because many factors will influence performance data after the implementation of a training program. The specific strategies in this step will pinpoint the amount of improvement directly related to the program. The result is increased accuracy and credibility of the ROI methodology results. Some commonly used strategies to address this important issue include:

➤ A pilot group of participants in a training program is compared with a control group not participating in the program to isolate program impact.

➤ Trend lines are used to project the values of specific output, and projections are compared with the actual data after a training program.

➤ A forecasting model projects output measures using the influence of other factors. The forecast is compared to actual measures. Mathematical relationships between input and output variables must be known for this approach to work.

➤ Participants/stakeholders estimate the amount of improvement related to a program.

➤ Supervisors and managers estimate the impact of a program on the output measures.

➤ External studies provide input about the impact of a program.

➤ Independent experts provide estimates of the impact of a program on the performance variable.

➤ When feasible, other influencing factors are identified, and the impact is estimated or calculated, leaving the remaining unexplained improvement attributable to the program.

➤ Customers provide input about the extent to which a program has influenced their decisions to use a product or service.

Collectively, these strategies provide a comprehensive set of tools to address the important and critical issue of isolating the effects of training and performance improvement programs.

## Convert Data to Monetary Values

To calculate the return on investment, practitioners convert business impact data to monetary values and compare those values to program costs. This requires a value be placed on each unit of data connected with the training and performance improvement programs. The list below shows most of the key strategies used to convert data to monetary values. The specific strategy selected depends on the type of data and the situation:

➤ *Output* data, such as an additional sale, are converted to profit contribution (or cost savings) and reported as a standard value.

➤ The cost of a *quality* measure, such as a customer complaint, is calculated and reported as a standard value.

➤ Employee *time* saved is converted to wages and benefits.

➤ *Historical costs* of preventing a measure, such as a lost time accident, are used when available.

➤ *Internal and external experts* estimate a value of a measure, such as an employee complaint.

➤ *External databases* contain an approximate value or cost of a data item, such as employee turnover.

➤ The measure is *linked to other measures* for which the costs are easily developed (e.g., employee satisfaction linked to turnover).

➤ *Participants estimate* the cost or value of the data item, such as work group conflict.

➤ *Supervisors or managers estimate* costs or values when they are willing and capable providing an estimate (e.g., an unscheduled absence).

➤ The training and performance improvement *staff estimates* a value of a data item, such as a sexual harassment complaint.

Converting data to monetary benefits is critical to determining the monetary benefits from training and performance improvement programs. The process is challenging, particularly with soft data, but can be methodically accomplished using one or more of these strategies.

## Capture Program Costs

The next step in the data analysis stage is capturing the costs of the program. Tabulating the costs involves monitoring or developing all of the costs related to the program. A fully-loaded cost profile is recommended when tabulating all direct and indirect costs (Marrelli 1993). Table 4.5 (at the end of this chapter) provides a sample cost summary detailing the fully-loaded costs necessary to maintain a conservative ROI calculation.

## Calculate the Return on Investment

As previously discussed, the return on investment is calculated by comparing the monetary benefits and the costs. The benefit-cost ratio is the monetary benefits of the program divided by the costs. In formula form it is:

$$BCR = \frac{\text{Program Benefits}}{\text{Program Costs}}$$

Sometimes this ratio is stated as a cost/benefit ratio, although the formula is the same as discussed earlier. The return on investment uses the *net* benefits divided by costs. The net benefits are program benefits minus the costs. In formula form, the ROI becomes:

$$ROI\% = \frac{\text{Net Program Benefits}}{\text{Program Costs}} \times 100$$

This is the same basic formula commonly used to evaluate other investments where the ROI is traditionally reported as earnings divided by investment.

The BCR and the ROI present the same general information but with slightly different perspectives. For example, say an effective meeting skills training program produced savings of $581,000, with a cost of $229,000. The benefit-cost ratio would be:

$$BCR = \frac{\$581{,}000}{\$229{,}000} = 2.54 \text{ (or 2.5:1)}$$

As this calculation shows, for every $1 invested in the training program, it returned approximately $2.50 in monetary benefits. To calculate the ROI, however, in this example, net benefits are $581,000 - $229,000=$352,000. Thus, the ROI is:

$$ROI\% = \frac{\$352{,}000}{\$229{,}000} \times 100 = 154\%$$

This means each $1 invested in the program returns approximately $1.50 in *net* benefits, after costs are covered. The benefits are usually expressed as annual benefits for short-term programs, representing the amount saved or gained for a complete year after the program has been implemented. Although the benefits may continue after the first year, the impact usually diminishes and is omitted from calculations in short-term situations. For long-term projects, the benefits are spread over several years.

## Identify Intangible Measures

In addition to tangible, monetary benefits, most training and performance improvement programs will derive intangible, non-monetary benefits. During data analysis, practitioners make every attempt to convert all data to monetary values. For example, hard data—such as output, quality, and time—are generally always converted to monetary values. Practitioners also must attempt to convert soft data. However, if the conversion process is too subjective or inaccurate and the resulting values lose credibility in the process, the data are labeled as intangible benefits with the appropriate explanation. For some programs, intangible, non-monetary benefits have extreme value, often commanding as much attention and influence as the hard data items (Moseley and Larson 1994). Intangible benefits include items such as:

➤ Improved public image;

➤ Increased job satisfaction;

➤ Increased organizational commitment;

➤ Enhanced technology leadership;

➤ Reduced stress;

➤ Improved teamwork;

➤ Improved customer service; or

➤ Reduced customer-response time.

## COMMUNICATE RESULTS

The final stage in the ROI methodology addresses the communication of results. This critical step includes several issues that are often neglected in the evaluation process. However, the communication process is often just as important as the evaluation itself. What information is reported and how the information is reported are important concerns.

There are five key reasons why communicating results effectively is so important.

1.  **Measurement and evaluation mean nothing without communication.** When the organization communicates the findings of a measurement and evaluation process to the appropriate audience, at the appropriate time, and in an effective manner, it creates a full loop from the program results to necessary actions based on those results.

2.  **Communicating results is necessary to make improvements.** During program evaluation, information is collected at different points in time. Providing feedback to the various groups each step along the way will allow for adjustments and provide the opportunity for improvements. Even after the program is complete, communication is necessary to

make sure the target audience understands the results achieved and how the results can be enhanced in future programs as well as in the current program. Communication is the key to making these important adjustments at all phases of the program.

3. **Communication is necessary to show accountability in programs.** Presenting results that encompass all six types of data will provide evidence of training's contribution to the organization, but can also be quite confusing. Different target audiences need different levels of explanation around results.

4. **Communication is a sensitive issue and can be the source of great benefit or the cause of major problems.** Because program results can be closely linked to political issues in an organization, communication can upset some individuals while pleasing others. If certain individuals do not receive the information or it is delivered inconsistently from one group to another, problems can quickly surface.

5. **A variety of target audiences need different information.** Given that there are so many potential target audiences for receiving communication about program success, it is important for the communication to be tailored directly to their needs. Planning and effort are necessary to make sure the audience receives all of the information it needs, in the proper format, and at the proper time. The scope, size, media, and even the actual information of different types and different levels will vary significantly from one group to another, making the target audience the key to determining the appropriate communication process.

Communicating results effectively is essential to the success of the ROI methodology. The next chapter outlines the necessary components of this crucial phase and discusses them in detail.

## TABLE 4.5

## FULLY-LOADED COST SUMMARY

**Analysis Costs**
Salaries and employee benefits – HRD staff
    (No. of people x average salary x employee benefits
    factor x hours on project)            _____
Meals, travel, and incidental expenses     _____
Office supplies and expenses     _____
Printing and reproduction     _____
Outside services     _____
Equipment expenses     _____
Registration fees     _____
General overhead allocation     _____
Other miscellaneous expenses     _____
**A. Total Analysis Costs**     _____

**Development Costs**
Salaries and employee benefits
    (No. of people x average salary x employee benefits
    factor x hours on project)     _____
Meals, travel, and incidental expenses     _____
Office supplies and expenses     _____
Program materials and supplies
    Film     _____
    Videotape     _____
    35mm slides     _____
    Overhead transparencies     _____
    Artwork     _____
    Manuals and materials     _____
    Other     _____
Printing and reproduction     _____
Outside services     _____
Equipment expenses     _____
General overhead allocation     _____
Other miscellaneous expenses     _____
**B. Total Development Costs**     _____

## TABLE 4.5

## FULLY-LOADED COST SUMMARY

**Delivery Costs**
Participant costs
    Salaries and employee benefits
    (No. of participants x average salary x employee
    benefits factor x training time)     _____
Instructor costs
    Salaries and benefits     _____
    Meals, travel, and incidental expenses     _____
    Outside services     _____
Meals, travel, and accommodations (No. of participants x
    average daily expenses x days of training)     _____
Program materials and supplies     _____
Participant replacement costs (if applicable)     _____
Lost production (explain basis)     _____
Facility costs
    Facilities rental     _____
    Facilities expenses allocation     _____
Equipment expenses     _____
General overhead allocation     _____
Other miscellaneous expenses     _____
**C. Total Delivery Costs**     _____

**Evaluation Costs**
Salaries and employee benefits – HRD staff
    (No. of people x average salary x employee
    benefits factor x hours on project)     _____
Meals, travel, and incidental expenses     _____
Participant cost     _____
Office supplies and expenses     _____
Printing and reproduction     _____
Outside services     _____
Equipment expenses     _____
General overhead allocation     _____
Other miscellaneous expenses     _____
**D. Total Evaluation Costs**     _____

**Total Program Costs (A + B + C + D)**     _____

Adapted from: Phillips, Jack J. 1997. *Return on Investment in Training and Performance Improvement Programs.* Boston: Butterworth-Heinemann.

## CHAPTER 5

# Stage 4: The Communication Process Model

*Communicating results is the last step* in the ROI methodology. But it is an important issue and one that deserves some attention. Communicating the results of a comprehensive measurement and evaluation should be systematic and well-planned, whether in hard

## FIGURE 5.1

### COMMUNICATION PROCESS MODEL

Analyze Need → Plan Communication → Assess Audience → Develop Report → Select Media → Present Results → Analyze Reactions →

Adapted from: Phillips, Jack J. 1997. *Handbook of Training Evaluation and Measurement Methods.* 3rd ed. Boston: Butterworth-Heinemann.

copy form, electronic form, or for an oral presentation. Figure 5.1 provides a model of the six components necessary to ensure effective communication takes place.

## ANALYZE NEED

The first step in the model is to analyze the need for the communication. There are many reasons why it's important to communicate the results of a program:

➤ To secure approval for training and performance improvements programs;

➤ To gain support for the training and performance improvement functions;

➤ To obtain commitment from participants in training and performance improvement programs;

➤ To build credibility for training and performance improvement programs;

➤ To reinforce the training and performance improvement processes;

➤ To explain the various issues around particular training and performance improvement programs;

➤ To demonstrate the importance of measuring training and performance improvement results;

➤ To market new and existing training and performance improvement programs;

➤ To satisfy clients' concerns regarding training and performance improvement;

➤ To improve training and performance improvement processes.

There are numerous other reasons why communicating the results of program evaluation is important. Each individual organization should review the specific reasons and tailor its communication strategy around those reasons.

# PLAN THE COMMUNICATION

Just as planning the evaluation process is important, so is planning the communication process. Thorough planning will ensure that the communication addresses both client concerns as well as issues important to the training and performance improvement staff and the general audience. Three issues are important in planning the communication of results:

➤ **Communication Guidelines**

➤ **Communication Around Specific Programs**

➤ **Communicating the ROI Impact Study**

## Communication Guidelines

When examining the complete training and performance improvement process, there should be guidelines for how the results will be communicated. These issues range from providing feedback during program implementation to communicating the ROI from an impact study. Seven areas should be considered in developing communication guidelines:

➤ **What will actually be communicated?**
It is important to detail the types of information communicated throughout the program.

➤ **When will the data be communicated?**
As with most projects and processes, timing is critical in communicating results.

➤ **How will the information be communicated?**
This shows the preferences toward particular types of communication media. For example, some organizations prefer to have written documents, while others prefer face-to-face meetings or electronic forms of communication.

83

➤ **Where will the communication take place?**

For some audiences, it may be more appropriate to present data in a formal on-site meeting; for others, it may be more appropriate to present data at an off-site, less formal location. The location is important in terms of convenience and perception.

➤ **Who will communicate the results?**

The messenger is another important issue to consider. Is it more appropriate for the training manager to present results? An independent third party? In any event, it is critical to consider the question when developing the overall communication strategy.

➤ **Who should receive the information?**

The identification of the target audience is another crucial issue. The client should receive the detailed report, or at the least, a presentation that reflects the detailed information. The general population of the organization should receive highlights. Ensuring that the appropriate audience receives the appropriate information is critical in achieving the desired response.

➤ **What actions are required or desired as a result of the communication?**

The final consideration in developing the communication plan is determining what actions are required or desired as a result of the communication. When communicating results to the training and performance improvement staff, changes may be necessary to the program. Communication to senior executives may be a call for a change in priorities in the training process. Clearly stating the desired outcomes of the communication is an important part of developing the overall strategy.

## Communication Around Specific Programs

When a specific program has been approved and the evaluation process is being planned, the communication plan is usually developed, along with the other evaluation planning documents. This details how specific information will be developed and communicated to various groups and the expected actions. In addition, this plan details how the overall results will be communicated, the time frames for communication, and the appropriate groups to receive information.

## Communicating the ROI Impact Study

The final issue regarding communication planning is the communication of the final ROI impact study. The presentation of this study occurs at the completion of the evaluation process when the results of all levels of evaluation have been analyzed. Different audiences need different levels of detail. For instance, the evaluation team and training staff will generally always receive a copy of the complete report. This complete report details the need for and objectives of the program, as well as the methodology used and the results of the evaluation. The results of the data collection (questionnaires, interview notes, focus groups notes, etc.) appear in an appendix.

When the evaluation process becomes routine, and senior and executive management are familiar with the process and the reporting format, a one-page summary of results can be used. This one-page report, as shown in table 5.1, provides the essential details and program results in a brief, bottomline format. A word of caution: while this report provides a quick look at the results, it is not advised to begin reporting results in this format until the evaluation process is well-supported within the organization and by senior and executive management. Also, as will be explained later, a formal presentation should be made to senior staff at least once to ensure they understand the process and that the results are perceived as credible.

Communication to other various audiences may come in the form of general interest overviews, general interest articles, and marketing materials. Some of these will be discussed in more detail later.

Table 5.2 is a sample communication plan. As shown, a complete report is provided for the client and the training staff. A much briefer

## TABLE 5.1

## SAMPLE STREAMLINED REPORT: ROI IMPACT STUDY

**Program Title:** Preventing Sexual Harassment at Healthcare, Inc.

**Target Audience:** First & Second Level Managers (655). Secondary: All employees through group meetings (6,844)

**Duration:** 1 day, 17 sessions

### RESULTS

**Level 1: Reaction**
➤ Overall rating 4.11 out of 5
➤ 93% provided action items

**Level 2: Learning**
➤ 65% increase post-test versus pre-test
➤ Skill practice demonstration

**Level 3: Application**
➤ 96% conducted meetings and completed meeting record
➤ 4.1 out of 5 on behavior change survey
➤ 68% report all action items complete
➤ 92% report some action items complete

**Level 4: Impact**
➤ Turnover Reduction: $2,840,632
➤ Complaint Reduction: $360,276
➤ Total Improvement: $3,200,908

**Level 5: ROI**
➤ 1,051%

**Intangible Benefits**
➤ Job Satisfaction
➤ Absenteeism
➤ Stress Reduction
➤ Image of HI
➤ Recruiting

**Technique to Isolate Effects of Program:** Trendline analysis; participant estimation

**Technique to Convert Data to Monetary Value:** Historical costs; internal experts

**Fully-loaded Program Costs:** $277,987

Source: Phillips, Patricia P. and Holly Burkett. 2001. *Managing Evaluation Shortcuts.* Infoline. Alexandria, VA: American Society for Training and Development.

report is provided for senior management. A general report is provided to participants. This step not only provides participants with program results, but also builds the credibility of the ROI methodology. Participants spend time completing questionnaires and participating in focus groups and interviews during the evaluation process. As part of their participation, they should be provided with the results.

A general interest article can be used for a company publication. This type of article keeps the accountability of training and performance improvement functions in front of the employees at large. Finally, the ROI results are published in marketing brochures to recruit new participants to the training and performance improvement program. The key is to plan the communication of the final impact study with the various report types and audiences in mind.

## TABLE 5.2

### COMMUNICATION PLAN

| Impact Study Report | Target Audience | Distribution Method |
|---|---|---|
| Complete report (100 pages) | Client team Training staff | Special meeting |
| Executive summary (8 pages) | Senior management | Routine meeting |
| General interest overview and summary (10 pages) | Participants | Mail with letter |
| General interest article (1 page) | All employees | Company newsletter |
| Brochure highlighting project, objectives, and specific results | Team leaders Other clients | Marketing materials |

Adapted from: Phillips, Jack J. 2000. *The Consultant's Scorecard: Tracking Results and Bottom-Line Impact of Consulting Projects.* New York: McGraw-Hill.

## ASSESS THE AUDIENCE

To the greatest extent possible, the training and performance improvement function should know its target audience for any communication. Understanding audience needs and issues will ensure that the function obtains the appropriate data from the evaluation process.

Along with understanding client needs and issues, there should also be a clear understanding of audience bias. While many will quickly support the program results, others will be skeptical or even resentful. Understanding and expecting these biases will assist in ensuring that the communication process can alleviate them. Some key questions to ask when assessing the audience are:

➤ Are they interested in the program?

➤ Do they want to receive the information?

➤ Has someone already made a commitment to them regarding communication?

➤ Is the timing right for this audience?

➤ Are they familiar with the program?

➤ How do they prefer to have results communicated?

➤ Are they likely to find the results threatening?

➤ Which medium will be most convincing to them?

## DEVELOP THE IMPACT STUDY REPORT

The next step in the communication process is the development of the final product of the comprehensive ROI evaluation—the impact study report. This report represents the complete results of the ROI methodology process. As mentioned previously, the impact study report provides the details of the evaluation along with supporting documents and summary results. The report is generally divided into three major sections: background information, results, and conclusions and recommendations.

## Background Information

This section gives an overview of the need for the program as well as a full description of the program. If applicable, the initial needs assessment is summarized. The description of the program includes program objectives, information on content, duration, course materials, facilitators, location, and other specific items.

---

**TABLE 5.3**

### SAMPLE TABLE OF CONTENTS

**ROI Impact Study**

**Table of Contents**
List of Tables
List of Figures
List of Exhibits

**Part I  Background Information**
Section 1:  Introduction
Section 2:  The Program
Section 3:  Model for Impact Study
Section 4:  Data Collection Strategy

**Part II  Results**
Section 5:  Reaction, Satisfaction, and Planned Action
Section 6:  Learning
Section 7:  Application and Implementation
Section 8:  Business Impact
Section 9:  Program Costs
Section 10:  ROI and Its Meaning
Section 11:  Intangible Benefits

**Part III  Conclusions and Recommendations**
Section 12:  Barriers and Enablers
Section 13:  Suggestions for Improvement
Section 14:  Conclusions
Section 15:  Recommendations

In this initial section, the evaluation process is described in detail as well. The description is detailed enough to ensure that the audience will understand the process, and that the evaluation process could be replicated based on the information in the report. Along with information on the process, the data collection strategy is detailed, including the instruments used, the timing of the data collection, and the sources of the data.

## Results

The next section presents the results of the evaluation. Beginning with Level 1, Reaction, and ending with intangible benefits, each of the six types of data generated through the ROI methodology are reported. This balanced set of measures is reported so that the entire story is told. While ROI is a critical measure in the reporting process, it is only one of six measures. By presenting the results in order, the audience can better understand the full impact of the program, not just on the bottomline, but on the participants, processes, and the organization as a whole.

## Conclusions and Recommendations

This section of the impact study report presents the conclusions and brief explanations of how each conclusion came about. The section also includes a list of recommendations for changes to the program with brief explanations. It is important that the conclusions and recommendations be consistent with one another and with the findings described in the previous section.

Table 5.3 provides a sample table of contents from an ROI impact study, representing these three major sections. A complete impact study can vary in length from 20–30 pages for a small project up to 200 or more pages for a very comprehensive evaluation. Remember that not all audiences need this detailed information. The key issue is to analyze the target audiences and develop a report that meets their specifications.

## SELECT MEDIA

There are many options available for communicating results. In addition to the actual report, the most frequently used media are meetings, interim and progress reports, organization publications, and case studies.

## Management Meetings

Management meetings are fertile ground for the communication of program results. All organizations have a variety of meetings, and in the proper context, program results can be an important part of each kind of meeting. The various management meetings include staff meetings, supervisory meetings, panel discussions, and management association meetings.

## Interim and Progress Reports

Interim and progress reports are brief reports mailed or e-mailed to the appropriate target audiences. A progress report could be something as simple as a "flash report" that appears when employees log on to e-mail. The employees have the option to read it when they log on initially or to save it for later reading.

## Organization Publications

Many organizations have newsletters or quarterly publications to keep employees abreast of the latest news and issues. Publishing program results in these publications can serve a number of purposes, including arousing general interest. A safety training program may be evaluated to determine its impact on lost-time accidents. When the evaluation finds that the program does indeed impact lost-time accidents, an article can highlight these results.

Stories about participants involved in a program and the results they achieve may help generate interest in the program by employees who would not have known about it otherwise. Reports of program success in organization publications can bring recognition to participants in the program. This public recognition can help build confidence and self-esteem in the individuals highlighted.

## Case Studies

Case studies are an effective way to communicate the results from a program evaluation. It is recommended that a few projects be developed in a case-study format. A typical case study will describe the situation, provide appropriate background information including the events that led to the program, present the techniques and strategies used to develop the study, and highlight the key issues in the program and the evaluation.

Case studies can be used in group discussions, allowing interested individuals to react to the material, offer different perspectives, and draw conclusions about approaches or techniques. They can serve as a self-teaching guide as individuals try to understand how evaluation is developed and used in the organization. They can also provide appropriate recognition for those who were involved in the actual case study or achieved the results.

The important issue is to understand which medium is most effective for the target audience and to include that decision in the overall communication strategy.

## PRESENT RESULTS

The next step is the actual presentation of results. There are generally two issues to consider.

### Providing Feedback

The first issue is the feedback provided throughout the training and performance improvement program being evaluated. This information is communicated primarily to the training and performance improvement staff and allows changes to be made during the program for continuous improvement.

### Presenting Results to Senior Management

The second issue to consider concerns communication to senior management. Two questions that should be asked when planning communication to this group are: "Do they believe you?" and "Can they take it?" By addressing these two concerns at the outset, they are not as big an issue when it's time to present the final results.

In responding to the first question, "Do they believe you?", the key is to ensure that when a program reaps a very large ROI, the presentation of the results includes all the steps covered in table 5.2. Beginning with the background of the program (as well as the ROI methodology) will build credibility for the evaluation process. Ensuring that the audience understands that efforts were made to be conservative in the evaluation will also build credibility. Also, presenting the results in order, beginning with Level 1 and building up to ROI and intangible benefits, will show senior management all the elements that go into the ROI. If the ROI is presented upfront, there's a risk the audience will not hear the rest of the presentation. Their focus will be on the end results, not the process.

The second question, "Can they take it?", refers to the fact that periodically, a program may result in a less than desirable or even negative ROI. While no one wants a negative ROI, the ROI methodology is not an individual performance evaluation—it is a process improvement tool. Negative ROIs can be invaluable sources of information on changes and improvements that need to be made—not only to training and performance improvement programs and processes, but to other processes throughout the organization. In communicating low or negative ROIs, follow the same outline in table 5.2. However, there should also be a plan for addressing the issues causing the negative ROI. If the program was too expensive, maybe it was inappropriate for the problem being addressed, meaning the needs assessment process may need to be adjusted. If there were barriers to implementing the skills learned and/or knowledge acquired during the program, those barriers should be addressed. If the program was just plain ineffective, kill it and move on to something more useful to employees and the organization. The important point is to view low and negative ROIs as an opportunity to make positive changes. When presenting these types of ROIs, be sure to present the plan for improvement or next steps.

## ANALYZE REACTIONS

A final step in the communication process is analyzing reactions to the communication. As with any process, evaluation of the communication process is critical to understanding where improvements are necessary. Communication is probably one of the most critical areas, yet little emphasis is placed on its evaluation. Analyzing reactions to communication will allow for improvements in future reports, presentations, and other communication processes. It will allow for any necessary changes in media or timing. It will help ensure that the key issues for different target audiences are covered and that the results of the ROI evaluation are clearly communicated to and understood by the various audiences.

During the presentation of results, questions may be asked or the information challenged. This input is important to remember for the next program evaluation. Compiling the questions can be useful in determining what types of information should be included in future communication. Positive comments should also be noted.

Training and performance improvement staff meetings are an excellent forum for discussing reactions to the presentation of results. Comments can come from many sources, depending on the particular target audiences. When a major presentation on program results is made, a feedback questionnaire may also be used on the entire audience. The purpose of this questionnaire is to determine the extent to which the audience understood and believed the information presented. Another approach to measuring reaction to the presentation of results is to conduct a survey of the management group to determine their perception of training and performance improvement programs.

## CHAPTER 6

# Overcoming Barriers and the Next Steps

Although progress is being made in the widespread implementation of ROI on training programs, there are still barriers which can inhibit implementation of the concept. Some of these barriers are realistic, while others are based on false perceptions. This section briefly describes the key barriers and ways to overcome them.

## COSTS AND TIME

A comprehensive measurement and evaluation process including ROI will add additional costs and time to the training or performance improvement program, although the added amount should not be excessive. The additional costs should be no more than 4 to 5 percent of the total training and performance improvement budget. The additional investment in ROI should be offset by the results achieved from implementation (e.g., the elimination or prevention of unproductive or unprofitable programs). The cost/time barrier alone stops many ROI implementations early in the process. However, there are a few short-cuts and cost savings approaches that can help to reduce the cost of the actual implementation (see table 6.1).

---

**TABLE 6.1**

**TIPS AND TECHNIQUES TO REDUCE THE COST OF IMPLEMENTING THE ROI PROCESS**

✓ Build evaluation into the performance improvement process.

✓ Develop criteria for selecting program measurement levels.

✓ Plan for evaluation early.

✓ Share responsibilities for evaluation.

✓ Require participants to conduct major steps.

✓ Use short-cut methods for major steps.

✓ Use estimates.

✓ Develop internal capability.

✓ Streamline the reporting process.

✓ Utilize technology.

---

Source: Phillips, Patricia P. and Holly Burkett. 2001. *Managing ROI Shortcuts*. Alexandria, VA: American Society for Training and Development.

## LACK OF SKILLS

Many staff members either do not understand ROI or don't have the skills necessary to apply the process within their scope of responsibilities. Also, the typical training program focuses more on qualitative feedback data than quantitative results. Consequently, a tremendous barrier to implementation is the discrepancy in the overall orientation, attitude, and skills of training and performance improvement staff members. Some suggestions for building skills in ROI include:

➤ Attending public workshops;

➤ Becoming certified in ROI implementation;

➤ Conducting internal workshops;

➤ Starting with less comprehensive evaluations and building skills;

➤ Participating in evaluation networking forums.

## FAULTY OR INADEQUATE INITIAL ANALYSIS

Many training and performance improvement programs do not have adequate initial analysis and assessment. Some functions implement programs for the wrong reasons, such as management requests or efforts to chase a popular fad or trend in the industry. If a program is not necessary or not based on business needs, it may not produce enough benefits to overcome the costs. An ROI calculation for an unnecessary program will likely yield a negative value. This is a realistic barrier for many programs. To overcome this barrier, develop or enhance the performance consulting process. Become engaged with the client in order to gain a deeper understanding of the needs. This will help ensure that the appropriate program or solution is implemented, yielding a greater ROI.

## FEAR

Some staff members do not pursue ROI because of fear of failure or fear of the unknown. Fear of failure appears in several ways. Some staff members will be concerned about the consequences of a negative ROI. They perceive the evaluation process as an individual performance evaluation rather than a process improvement tool. For others, a comprehensive measurement process can stir up the traditional fear of change and all the unknown it brings. Although often based on unrealistic assumptions and a lack of knowledge of the process, fear is so strong that it becomes a real barrier to many ROI implementations. Making sure staff members understand the process and its intent is key to dissolving this fear.

## DISCIPLINE AND PLANNING

Successful implementation of the ROI methodology requires significant planning and a disciplined approach to keep the process on track. It requires implementation schedules, transition plans, evaluation targets,

ROI analysis plans, measurement and evaluation policies, and follow-up schedules. The practitioner may not have enough discipline and determination to stay the course. This inevitably becomes a barrier, particularly when there is no immediate pressure to measure the ROI. If clients or other executives are not demanding ROI evaluation, the staff may not allocate the necessary time for planning and coordination. Also, other pressures and priorities often eat into the time necessary for ROI implementation. Planning the work and working from the plan is key to successful implementation.

## FALSE ASSUMPTIONS

Many professionals have false assumptions about ROI that deter them from pursuing implementation. Typical false assumptions include:

➤ ROI can only be applied to a few narrowly focused programs.

➤ Senior managers do not want to see the results of programs expressed in monetary values.

➤ If clients do not ask for ROI, it should not be pursued.

➤ If the CEO does not ask for ROI, then he or she does not expect it.

While these assumptions are usually based on incorrect data or misunderstandings, they still form realistic barriers that impede the progress of ROI implementation. Again, understanding the methodology and the need for ROI are critical factors in overcoming this barrier.

## GETTING TO THE NEXT STEPS

Now that the ROI methodology has been explained along with the various pieces of the evaluation puzzle, the question is "What now?" How does one get started evaluating programs using the ROI methodology? The previous section covering implementation issues provides some insight. However, as a focused review, table 6.2 provides a check list of steps to help newcomers to the ROI methodology begin their implementation process. As progress is made and issues surface, there are numerous sources available to assist in implementing ROI. Many of those sources are listed in the reference section at the back of the book.

## TABLE 6.2

### ROI IMPLEMENTATION: GETTING STARTED

**Implementing ROI**

- ❑ Assess progress and readiness for ROI implementation.
- ❑ Organize a taskforce or network to initiate the process.
- ❑ Develop and publish a philosophy or mission statement concerning accountability and ROI of all training and performance improvement programs.
- ❑ Clarify roles and responsibilities of task force members.
- ❑ Develop a transition plan detailing the steps necessary to successfully implement ROI.
- ❑ Set targets for evaluating programs at the various levels of evaluation.
- ❑ Develop guidelines to ensure that ROI is implemented completely and consistently.
- ❑ Build staff skills.
- ❑ Establish a management support system or champions of ROI.
- ❑ Enhance management support and commitment throughout communication and their participation in the implementation of ROI.
- ❑ Achieve short-term results by evaluating "one program at a time."
- ❑ Communicate results to selective audiences.
- ❑ Teach the process to others to enhance their understanding of ROI.
- ❑ Establish a quality review process to ensure that the evaluation process remains consistent and credible.

## THE BOTTOMLINE

So what is the bottomline on ROI? The ROI methodology is a fundamentally sound process that has been used for generations to show the value of programs, projects, and processes within organizations. The ROI calculation is the financial ratio used by accountants, chief financial officers, and executives to measure the return on all investments. The term ROI is already familiar to all executives and operational managers. It is not a new fly-by-night catch phrase with an unknown meaning that can only be explained through elaborate presentations and is only understood in a very small area of the organization.

ROI as described in this book goes beyond a cost-benefit comparison. Rather it provides a balanced viewpoint of the impact of training and performance improvement programs, by taking into consideration participant reaction, learning, application of new skills and knowledge, and business impact achieved through the programs. The methodology presents the complete picture of program success. Further, by including the critical step of isolating the effects of the program, the impact to business can be further linked to training and performance improvement programs. The process presented in this book is based on sound research and conservative guidelines. Although not all programs should be evaluated at the ROI level, for those meeting specific criteria, ROI is a credible approach to providing evidence of the training and performance improvement program's financial impact on the organization. A thorough and complete understanding of ROI can help eliminate fears and overcome barriers to its implementation.

# APPENDIX

## APPENDIX 1

## IS YOUR ORGANIZATION A CANDIDATE FOR ROI IMPLEMENTATION?

Read each question and check off the most appropriate level of agreement on a scale of 1 to 5 (1 = Total Disagreement; 5 = Total Agreement).

| | Disagree | | | Agree | |
|---|---|---|---|---|---|
| | 1 | 2 | 3 | 4 | 5 |
| 1. My organization is considered a large organization with a wide variety of training and performance improvement programs. | ☐ | ☐ | ☐ | ☐ | ☐ |
| 2. We have a large training and performance improvement budget that reflects the interest of senior management. | ☐ | ☐ | ☐ | ☐ | ☐ |
| 3. Our organization has a culture of measurement and is focused on establishing a variety of measures including training and performance improvement. | ☐ | ☐ | ☐ | ☐ | ☐ |
| 4. My organization is undergoing significant change. | ☐ | ☐ | ☐ | ☐ | ☐ |
| 5. There is pressure from senior management to measure results of our training and performance improvement programs. | ☐ | ☐ | ☐ | ☐ | ☐ |
| 6. My training and performance improvement function currently has a very low investment in measurement and evaluation. | ☐ | ☐ | ☐ | ☐ | ☐ |
| 7. My organization has experienced more than one program disaster in the past. | ☐ | ☐ | ☐ | ☐ | ☐ |
| 8. My organization has a new training and performance improvement leader. | ☐ | ☐ | ☐ | ☐ | ☐ |
| 9. My team would like to be the leaders in training and performance improvement processes. | ☐ | ☐ | ☐ | ☐ | ☐ |
| 10. The image of our training and performance improvement function is less than satisfactory. | ☐ | ☐ | ☐ | ☐ | ☐ |

## APPENDIX 1

## IS YOUR ORGANIZATION A CANDIDATE FOR ROI IMPLEMENTATION?

|  | Disagree 1 2 | Agree 3 4 5 |
|---|---|---|
| 11. My clients are demanding that our training and performance improvement processes show bottom-line results. | ❑ ❑ | ❑ ❑ ❑ |
| 12. My training and performance improvement function competes with other functions within our organization for resources. | ❑ ❑ | ❑ ❑ ❑ |
| 13. There is increased focus on linking training and performance improvement processes to the strategic direction of the organization. | ❑ ❑ | ❑ ❑ ❑ |
| 14. My training and performance improvement function is a key player in change initiatives currently taking place in my organization. | ❑ ❑ | ❑ ❑ ❑ |
| 15. Our overall training and performance improvement budget is growing, and we are required to prove the bottom-line value of our processes. | ❑ ❑ | ❑ ❑ ❑ |

## SCORING

If you scored:

**15–30** You are not yet a candidate for ROI.

**31–45** You are not a strong candidate for ROI. However, it is time to start pursuing some type of measurement process.

**46–60** You are a candidate for building skills to implement the ROI methodology. At this point there is no real pressure to show the ROI, which is the best time to perfect the process within the organization.

**61–75** You should already be implementing a comprehensive measurement and evaluation process including ROI.

Adapted from: Phillips, Jack J., Ron Stone, and Patricia P. Phillips. 2001. *The Human Resources Scorecard: Measuring the Return on Investment.* Boston: Butterworth-Heinemann.

## APPENDIX 2

## FULLY-LOADED COST SUMMARY

**Analysis Costs**

Salaries and employee benefits – HRD staff
   (No. of people x average salary x employee benefits
   factor x hours on project)                                      _____
Meals, travel, and incidental expenses                            _____
Office supplies and expenses                                      _____
Printing and reproduction                                         _____
Outside services                                                  _____
Equipment expenses                                                _____
Registration fees                                                 _____
General overhead allocation                                       _____
Other miscellaneous expenses                                      _____
**A. Total Analysis Costs**                                       _____

**Development Costs**

Salaries and employee benefits
   (No. of people x average salary x employee benefits
   factor x hours on project)                                      _____
Meals, travel, and incidental expenses                            _____
Office supplies and expenses                                      _____
Program materials and supplies
   Film                                                           _____
   Videotape                                                      _____
   35mm slides                                                    _____
   Overhead transparencies                                        _____
   Artwork                                                         _____
   Manuals and materials                                          _____
   Other                                                           _____
Printing and reproduction                                         _____
Outside services                                                  _____
Equipment expenses                                                _____
General overhead allocation                                       _____
Other miscellaneous expenses                                      _____
**B. Total Development Costs**                                     _____

## APPENDIX 2

## FULLY-LOADED COST SUMMARY

**Delivery Costs**

Participant costs
    Salaries and employee benefits
    (No. of participants x average salary x employee
    benefits factor x training time)    _____
Instructor costs
    Salaries and benefits    _____
    Meals, travel, and incidental expenses    _____
    Outside services    _____
Meals, travel, and accommodations (No. of participants x
    average daily expenses x days of training)    _____
Program materials and supplies    _____
Participant replacement costs (if applicable)    _____
Lost production (explain basis)    _____
Facility costs
    Facilities rental    _____
    Facilities expenses allocation    _____
Equipment expenses    _____
General overhead allocation    _____
Other miscellaneous expenses    _____
**C. Total Delivery Costs**    _____

**Evaluation Costs**

Salaries and employee benefits – HRD staff
    (No. of people x average salary x employee
    benefits factor x hours on project)    _____
Meals, travel, and incidental expenses    _____
Participant cost    _____
Office supplies and expenses    _____
Printing and reproduction    _____
Outside services    _____
Equipment expenses    _____
General overhead allocation    _____
Other miscellaneous expenses    _____
**D. Total Evaluation Costs**    _____

**Total Program Costs (A + B + C + D)**    _____

Adapted from: Phillips, Jack J. 1997. *Return on Investment in Training and Performance Improvement Programs.* Boston: Butterworth-Heinemann.

# References

Alampay, R. H., and F. T. Morgan. 2000. Evaluating external executive education at Dow Chemical. *Human Resource Development International* 3, no. 4: 489-498.

Alliger, G. M., and S. I. Tannenbaum. 1997. A meta-analysis of the relations among training criteria. *Personnel Psychology* 50, no. 2: 341-358.

American Productivity and Quality Center (APQC). 2000. *The corporate university: Measuring the impact of learning.* Houston, Texas: American Productivity & Quality Center.

Anthony, Robert N., and J. S. Reece. 1983. *Accounting text and cases.* New York: Irwin.

Benson, D. K., and V.P. Tran. 2002. Workforce development ROI. In *Measuring return on investment in the public sector*, edited by Patricia P. Phillips. Alexandria, Virginia: American Society for Training and Development.

Broad, Mary L., and John W. Nestrom. 1992. *Transfer of training.* Boston: Perseus Books.

Foshay, W. 1998. Choosing a strategy for return on investment justification. *Performance Improvement* (October): 6-8.

Galvin, T. 2001. Birds of a feather. *Training* 38, no. 3: 57-88.

Gerson, G., and C. McCleskey. 1998. Numbers help make a training decision that counts. *HR Magazine* (July): 51-58.

Hill, D. 1997. Preventing sexual harassment. In *Measuring return on investment volume 2*, edited by Jack J. Phillips. In Action Series. Alexandria, Virginia: American Society for Training and Development.

Hornegren, Charles T. 1982. *Cost accounting.* Englewood Cliffs, New Jersey: Prentice Hall.

Kearsley, Greg. 1982. *Costs, benefits, & productivity in training systems.* Reading, Massachusetts: Addison-Wesley Publishing.

Kirkpatrick, Donald L. 1994. *Evaluating training programs: The four levels.* San Francisco: Berrett-Koehler Publishers.

Malecki, Edward J. 1997. *Technology & economic development.* London: Addison Wesley Longman.

Marrelli, A. F. 1993. Cost analysis for training. *Technical Skills Training* 4, no. 8: 8-14.

Moseley, J. L., and S. Larson. 1994. A qualitative application of Kirkpatrick's model for evaluation workshops and conferences. *Performance & Instruction* 33, no. 8: 3-5.

Nas, T. F. 1996. *Cost-benefit analysis.* Thousand Oaks, California: Sage Publications.

Phillips, Jack J. 1995. Corporate training: Does it pay off? *William & Mary Business Review* (summer): 6-10.

———. 1996a. Was it the training? *Training and Development* (March): 28-32.

———. 1996b. How much is the training worth? *Training and Development* (April): 20-24.

———. 1997a. *Return on investment in training and performance improvement programs.* Boston: Butterworth-Heinemann.

———. 1997b. *Handbook of training evaluation and measurement methods.* 3rd ed. Boston: Butterworth-Heinemann.

———. 1999. *HRD trends worldwide: Shared solutions to compete in a global economy.* Boston: Butterworth-Heinemann.

———. 2000. *The consultant's scorecard.* New York: McGraw-Hill.

———, ed. 1994. *Measuring return on investment Volume 1.* In Action Series. Alexandria, Virginia: American Society for Training and Development.

————, ed. 1997c. *Measuring Return on Investment Volume 2*. In Action Series. Alexandria, Virginia: American Society for Training and Development.

Phillips, Jack J., and Patricia P. Phillips. 2000. The return-on-investment process: Issues and trends. *Training Journal* (October): 8-12.

Phillips, Jack J., Ron D. Stone, and Patricia P. Phillips. 2001. *The human resources scorecard: Measuring the return on investment*. Boston: Butterworth-Heinemann.

Phillips, Patricia P., ed. 2001. *Measuring Return on Investment Volume 3*. In Action Series, edited by Jack J. Phillips. Alexandria, Virginia: American Society for Training and Development.

————, ed. 2002. *Return on investment in the public sector*. In Action Series, edited by Jack J. Phillips. Alexandria, Virginia: American Society for Training and Development.

Phillips, Patricia P., and Holly Burkett. 2001. *Managing Evaluation Shortcuts*. Infoline. Alexandria, Virginia: American Society for Training and Development.

Phillips, Patricia P., and Holly Burkett. 2001. *Managing ROI Shortcuts*. Alexandria, Virginia: American Society for Training and Development.

Schmidt, W. 1997. Cost-benefit analysis techniques for training investments. *Technical & Skills Training* (April): 18-21.

Sibbett, D. 1997. Harvard Business Review: 75 years of management ideas and practice 1922-1977. *Harvard Business Review*.

Thompson, Mark S. 1980. *Benefit-cost analysis for program evaluation*. Thousand Oaks, California: Sage Publications.

*Training*. 2000. Industry Report 2000. *Training* 37, no. 10 (October): 45-55.

*Training*. 2001. Industry Report 2001. *Training* 38, no. 10 (October): 40-75.

Van Buren, M. 2001. *State of the Industry Report 2001.* Alexandria, Virginia: American Society for Training and Development (51).

Warr, Peter, Catriona Allan, and Kamal Birdi. 1999. Predicting three levels of training outcome. *Journal of Occupational and Organizational Psychology* 72: 351-375.

Willmore, J. 2001. Trends in the profession. In *What smart trainers know*, edited by Lorraine L. Ukens. San Francisco: Jossey-Bass/Pfieffer.

# Index

Accountability 23, 24, 35

Behavior changes
  measuring 45
Benefit-cost ratio 74
Business impact 66

Case studies 43, 53, 54
  using to communicate results
    91–92
Communicating results 64,
    76–77, 81–94
  developing communication
    guidelines 83–84
Communication process model
    81–94
  analyzing need 82–83
  analyzing reactions 93
  assessing audience 88
  developing communication
    guidelines 83–84
  developing impact study report
    88–90
  presenting results 92–93
  selecting media 90
Cost-benefit analysis 18, 35, 46

Cost-benefit ratio 74
Costs
  calculating 74
  historical 73
  of ROI 95
Credibility 60
  enhancing 51

Data analysis 57, 64, 71–76
  calculating ROI 74–75
  capturing costs 74
  converting data to monetary
    value 72–73
  identifying intangible measures
    75–76
  isolating program effects 71–72
Data collection 57, 64, 70–71
  methods for 70–71
  plan 68, 69

Evaluation framework 43, 45–49
  Kirkpatrick's levels 45–49
  Phillips' levels 46–47
Evaluation plan
  developing 66–70

Evaluation planning  64–70
   developing evaluation plan
      66–70
   developing program objectives
      64–66
Evaluation Puzzle  43–58
Executive summary  57

Hard data  62, 75

Impact study  57
   communicating results  57,
      85–87
Impact study report
   developing  88–90
Implementation  53–58
   assigning responsibilities  55
   briefing managers  58
   developing plan  55–58
   developing skills  55
   preparing guidelines  58
Intangible benefits  75–76
Isolating program effects  46, 51,
      63, 68, 71–72, 100

Job performance  66

Kirkpatrick, Donald  45

Learning  66
   measuring  45

Management meetings
   using to communicate results  91

Net benefits  19, 30, 74
Newsletters
   using to communicate results  91

Operating standards and guidelines
      43, 49–53
Output data  73

Participant satisfaction  66
Performance improvement
   and ROI  17
Performance improvement
      programs
   budgets  17
   increase in  28
   changes in  21–22
   fully-loaded costs  62
   linking to strategic initiatives  24
   weeding out ineffective programs
      24
Phillips, Jack  46–47, 63
Program objectives
   business  66
   job performance  66
   learning  66
   participant satisfaction  66
Progress reports
   using to communicate results  91
Project plan
   developing  56–57

Quality measure  73

Reaction
   measuring  45
Resources
   at risk  23
   competition for  23
Results
   measuring  45
ROI analysis plan  68

ROI calculation 18, 74–75, 100
  for unnecessary programs 97
ROI methodology 45, 100
  barriers to implementation
    95–100
  benefits of 30–33
  building skills in 96–97
  costs and time 95
  criteria checklist 63
  criteria for 60–62
  false assumptions about 98
  handling negative results 93
  issues driving 22–30
  model 50, 65
  savings with 32
  self-checklist 41–42, 102–3
  symptoms indicating need for
    38–40
  target audiences 59–60

ROI model 43, 49
ROI ratio 46

Soft data 62, 75
Strategic initiatives
  linking training to 24

Training
  and ROI 17
  budgets 17, 37
    increase in 28, 29
  changes in 21–22
  delivery 22
  fully-loaded costs 62
  linking to strategic initiatives 24
  soft-skills 22
  weeding out ineffective programs
    24

# About the Author

### Patricia Pulliam Phillips

Patricia is Chairman & CEO of The Chelsea Group, a research and consulting company focused on accountability issues in training, HR, and performance improvement. Patricia conducts research on accountability issues and works with clients to build accountability systems and processes in their organizations. She has helped organizations implement the ROI methodology, developed by Jack J. Phillips, in countries around the world. She has been involved in hundreds of ROI impact studies in a variety of industries.

Patricia has over 13 years experience in the electrical utility industry. As manager of a market planning and research organization, she was responsible for the development of marketing programs for residential, commercial, and industrial customers. Patricia also played an integral role in establishing Marketing University, a learning environment that supported the needs of new sales and marketing representatives.

Patricia has a Master of Arts Degree in Public and Private Management from Birmingham-Southern College. She is certified in ROI evaluation and serves as co-author on the subject in publications including *Corporate University Review, The Journal of Lending and Credit Risk Management, Training Journal, What Smart Trainers Know,* and *Evaluating Training Programs,* 2nd Edition, by Donald L. Kirkpatrick. Patricia has authored and co-authored several issues of the American Society for Training and Development *Infoline* Series including *Mastering ROI* and *ROI on a Shoestring.* She served as Issue Editor for the ASTD *In Action* casebook, *Measuring Return on*

*Investment Volume 3*, and *Measuring Return on Investment in the Public Sector*. Patricia is co-author of *The Human Resources Scorecard: Measuring Return on Investment*. Patricia may be reached at TheChelseaGroup@aol.com.

# About the Series Editor

*Jack J. Phillips, Ph.D.*
*Jack Phillips Center for Research, a division of Franklin Covey*
As a world-renowned expert on measurement and evaluation, Dr. Jack J. Phillips provides consulting services for Fortune 500 companies and conducts workshops at major HR and training conferences throughout the world. Phillips is also the author or editor of more than thirty books—ten about measurement and evaluation—and more than one hundred articles.

His expertise in measurement and evaluation is based on more than twenty-seven years of corporate experience in five industries. Phillips has served as training and development manager at two Fortune 500 firms, senior HR officer at two firms, president of a regional federal savings bank, and management professor at a major state university.

His background in training and HR led Phillips to develop the ROI methodology—a revolutionary process that provides bottom-line figures and accountability for all types of training, performance improvement, human resources, and technology programs.

In 1992, Phillips founded Performance Resources Organization (PRO), an international consulting firm that provides comprehensive assessment, measurement, and evaluation services for organizations. In 1999, PRO was acquired by the Franklin Covey Company and is now known as The Jack Phillips Center for Research. The Center is a leading provider of measurement and evaluation services to the global business community. Phillips consults with clients in manufacturing, service, and government organizations in countries throughout the world.

Books most recently authored by Phillips include *The Human Resources Scorecard: Measuring the Return on Investment, The Consultant's Scorecard, HRD Trends Worldwide: Shared Solutions to Compete in a Global Economy, Return on Investment in Training and Performance Improvement Programs, Handbook of Training Evaluation and Measurement Methods,* 3rd edition, and *Accountability in Human Resource Management.* Phillips is series editor for ASTD's In Action casebook series, Butterworth-Heinemann's Improving Human Performance series, and the Measurement in Action series published by CEP Press.

Phillips has undergraduate degrees in electrical engineering, physics, and mathematics from Southern Polytechnic State University and Oglethorpe University, a master's degree in decision sciences from Georgia State University, and a Ph.D. in human resource management from the University of Alabama. In 1987 he won the Yoder-Heneman Personnel Creative Application Award from the Society for Human Resource Management.

**Join ISPI Today!**

**International Society for Performance Improvement (ISPI)** *is the leading international association of professionals who are dedicated to improving individual, organizational and societal performance.*

ISPI members hold management and line positions in performance technology, employee training, human resource development, instructional design, organizational development and other key management areas.

For four decades, ISPI members have been steadily improving performance for the largest, most successful organizations in some 40 countries around the World.

Individual ISPI members are employed by private firms and corporations (including 75% of the Fortune 100), leading educational institutions, non-profit organizations, and numerous city, state and provincial governments, as well as national civilian and military agencies of countries around the World.

ISPI corporate members and supporters include Arthur Andersen, CADDI, Comcast Cable, Eli Lilly, Ford Motor Company, Georgia-Pacific, Hewlett Packard, IBM, iGeneration, International Monetary Fund, Maritz, Metropolitan Life Insurance, Microsoft, Sun Microsystems, United States Coast Guard, United States Food and Drug Administration, Walgreen, Wells Fargo and others.

**ISPI offers its members performance improvement education and networking through conferences, institutes, book publishing, professional journals, an interactive Website, research, and local chapters.**

For more information about ISPI:

International Society for Performance Improvement

1400 Spring Street, Suite 260

Silver Spring, Maryland 20910 USA

Telephone: 1.301.587.8570

Fax: 1.301.587.8573

E-mail: info@ispi.org

Web: www.ispi.org

*Experience ISPI…Experience Value!*

Name _____

Title _____

Organization _____

Mailing Address _____

City _____

State/Province _____

Zip/Post Code _____

Country _____

Phone _____

Fax _____

E-mail _____

Credit Card # _____

❏ VISA  ❏ MasterCard  ❏ AMEX

Exp. Date _____

Signature _____

| Membership Fees | | $ US |
|---|---|---|

If you are outside the US or Canada, please see the supplemental postage charges below.

| | | |
|---|---|---|
| Active Member (includes $69 for PI) | $ 145 | $ |
| Student Member (Attach proof of full-time student status.) | $ 60 | $ |
| Retired Member | $ 60 | $ |
| Patron Member | $1,400 | $ |
| Sustaining Member | $ 950 | $ |

**Special New Member Offer**

| | | |
|---|---|---|
| *The Handbook of Human Performance Technology* (Regularly $84.95) | $ 70 | $ |

Subscription charges

| *Performance Improvement Quarterly (PIQ)* | | |
|---|---|---|
| Active Member | $ 40 | $ |
| Student/Retired Member | $ 22 | $ |
| Commercial/Library Subscription | $ 64 | $ |

| *Performance Improvement (PI)* | | |
|---|---|---|
| Non-Member Subscription | $ 69 | $ |
| Commercial/Library Subscription | $ 69 | $ |

**Supplemental Postage Charges**

| | | |
|---|---|---|
| Members and *PI* Subscribers Outside USA or Canada | $ 50 | $ |
| *PIQ* Subscribers Outside USA or Canada | $ 20 | $ |

| **Your Total Investment** | $ |
|---|---|